STUDENT LEADERS:
GROWING FROM STUDENTS TO CEOS

STUDENT LEADERS: GROWING FROM STUDENTS TO CEOS

PROFESSOR M.S.RAO, Ph.D.
INTERNATIONAL LEADERSHIP GURU

STUDENT LEADERS:
GROWING FROM STUDENTS TO CEOS
By Professor M.S.Rao

Printing History:

First Print: June 2013

ISBN 13: 978-93-5110-163-5

Published by Shroff Publishers & Distributors Pvt. Ltd. C-103, T.T.C. Industrial Area, M.I.D.C., Pawane, Navi Mumbai - 400 705. Tel.: (91-22) 4158 4158 Fax: (91-22) 4158 4141 E-mail: spdorders@shroffpublishers.com. Printed at Repro India. Ltd. Mahape Navi Mumbai.

International Acclaim for Professor M.S.Rao's Book!

"The international leadership guru, Professor M.S. Rao has come out with yet another leadership book *Student Leaders: Growing From Students to CEOs*. This book assists students to shift successfully from campus to corporate as leaders and unfolds 21 timeless tools to become CEOs. I strongly recommend reading this book."

Vijay Govindarajan
World's Third-Ranked Management Guru

"In this new book, Professor M.S. Rao focuses on the future by drawing inspiration and wisdom from the past—including the insights of Swami Vivekananda. Professor Rao presents knowledge as the key to personal and social transformation that can make the world a better, safer place. He demonstrates his commitment to advancing the intellectual and spiritual development of our youth by providing a framework that fosters leadership through reflection and personal growth. Professor Rao's enthusiasm for his subject makes this an engaging text, especially for students looking to develop a leadership mindset and associated skills."

Dipak C. Jain,
Dean, INSEAD

"A native of India, Professor M. S. Rao has written his 20th book, *Student Leaders: Growing From Students To CEOs* which is destined to become a worldwide phenomenon on student leadership. Students and teachers from every country should take good notes in this course to prepare future leaders and CEOs; it offers a syllabus for success in the corporate world."

Marshall Goldsmith
The Thinkers50 Award Winner (sponsored by Harvard Business Review) for Most-Influential Leadership Thinker in the World

"The global management thinker Professor M.S. Rao has come out with yet another leadership book entitled *Student Leaders: Growing From Students to CEOs*, unveiling 11 success sutras for students. I highly recommend this book for all students who aspire to successful careers."

Patricia Wheeler, Ph.D.
Global Executive Coach,
Managing Partner, The Levin Group LLC

"Renowned leadership thinker Professor M.S. Rao has made an important contribution to the study of leadership development with the release of *Student Leaders: Growing from Students to CEOs*. The world needs more leaders! Most leadership development, though, is aimed at middle-aged who are less impressionable than those from younger generations. Student Leaders shows how to reach this untapped potential, and how to convert the energy and enthusiasm of budding young leaders, into strong and seasoned leadership influence. Bravo Professor M.S. Rao!"

Bill Treasurer,
Author, Leaders Open Doors and Courage Goes to Work

"Professor M.S.Rao's new book, *Student Leaders: Growing From Students to CEOs*, is an important resource for those wanting to get on the path of success early. Packed with the wisdom of international leaders and Professor Rao's practical and immediately applicable advice, young leaders can learn from the successes and failures of others in an entertaining and easy to digest read."

Harrison Monarth,
New York Times bestselling author of The Confident Speaker, author of 360 Degrees of Influence

"The global management guru, Professor M.S. Rao has come out with yet another leadership book *Student Leaders: Growing From Students to CEOs*. It unveils 11 success sutras for students to grow as leaders and CEOs. I strongly recommend reading this book."

Chris Widener
Author, the Art of Influence

"As a leadership educator and a day-to-day practitioner, I have always found Professor M.S. Rao's work both practical and impactful. This is another great example, with a series of thoughtful yet perceptive ideas aimed to help aspiring leaders at all levels to be the best they can be. Highly recommended."

Mick Yates
Visiting Professor, University of Leeds and Founder, LeaderValues

"The global leadership guru, Professor M.S. Rao has come out with yet another leadership book, *Student Leaders: Growing From Students to CEOs.* It introduces an alternative leadership perspective - 'Soft Leadership' and substantiates that Mahatma Gandhi was a soft leader. It is must read."

Bob Urichuck,
International Professional Speaker, Trainer and Author of Up Your Bottom Line, Velocity Selling and Disciplined for Life.

"Professor M.S. Rao nails it again! He knows that the seeds of leadership need to be planted and sown early on to groom future leaders. Campus leadership programs must facilitate the kind of self-awareness that is so crucial to leadership success. Professor Rao not only makes the case, but provides a blueprint to make it happen, offering us the bonus of inspirational quotes from his personal heroes."

Dr. Lois J. Zachary
President, Leadership Development Services, LLC

"The international leadership expert and speaker, Professor M.S. Rao has come out with yet another leadership book for students, *Student Leaders: Growing From Students to CEOs.* This book contains interesting case studies, stories, anecdotes, and illustrations based on author's 32 years of experiences in various capacities. It calls upon students to build leadership skills and excel as CEOs."

Lenny Laskowski
Author of Painless Presentations- the Proven Stress-free way to Successful Public Speaking

"Professor M. S. Rao is a well sought after and internationally renowned speaker & author. His book contains very down-to-earth and practical methods for students to take to achieve success as leaders in the corporate arena. This is a must-read for anyone who wants to become a corporate leader."

Jeffrey Lim
Vice President, Compliance & Regulation
Walton Berhad

"International management thinker, Professor M.S. Rao's book is full of good ideas for students to learn about becoming a leader. Two ideas best define what leadership is: 'Inspire people with what you have and by giving what they want.' and 'Acquire the requisite attitude, skills and knowledge and share them with others.' Students at all ages can begin to use these as they move through school and into the world of business."

Alan J. Zell
Ambassador Of Selling, Attitudes for Selling
Winner of the Murray Award for Marketing Excellence

Quotes

"The foundation of every state is the education of its youth." - **Diogenes Laertius**

The young do not know enough to be prudent, and therefore they attempt the impossible - and achieve it, generation after generation." - **Pearl S. Buck**

"Keep your dreams alive. Understand to achieve anything requires faith and belief in yourself, vision, hard work, determination, and dedication. Remember all things are possible for those who believe." - **Gail Devers**

"A good teacher is someone who examines everything he teaches. Old ideas can't enslave men because, with time, they have to be adapted and be given new shapes. So let us take the philosophical riches of the past and keep in mind all challenges the present world offers us." - **Confucius**

"All differences in this world are of degree, and not of kind, because oneness is the secret of everything." - **Swami Vivekananda**

“If one advances confidently in the direction of his dreams, and endeavors to live the life which he has imagined, he will meet with success unexpected in common hours.” - **Henry David Thoreau**

"Words do two major things: They provide food for the mind and create light for understanding and awareness."— **Jim Rohn**

“If you understand others you are smart.
If you understand yourself you are illuminated.
If you overcome others you are powerful.
If you overcome yourself you have strength.
If you know how to be satisfied you are rich.
If you can act with vigor, you have a will.
If you don't lose your objectives you can be long-lasting.”
– **Lao Tzu**

“I am proud to belong to a religion which has taught the world tolerance and universal acceptance.” – **Swami Vivekananda.**

"Mix a little mystery with everything, for mystery arouses veneration." — **Baltasar Gracián**

"Charisma is a sparkle in people that money can't buy. It's an invisible energy with visible effects."— **Marianne Williamson**

"A teacher's purpose is not to create students in his own image, but to develop students who can create their own image." - **Author Unknown**

"To succeed in your mission, you must have single-minded devotion to your goal." - **Abdul Kalam**

"If you hear a voice within you say 'you cannot paint,' then by all means paint, and that voice will be silenced." – **Vincent Van Gogh**

"Don't go around saying the world owes you a living. The world owes you nothing. It was here first." –Mark Twain

"Success consists of going from failure to failure without loss of enthusiasm." –**Winston Churchill**

"Your time is limited, don't waste it living someone else's life. Don't be trapped by dogma, which is living the result of other people's thinking. Don't let the noise of other's opinion drowned your own inner voice. And most important, have the courage to follow your heart and intuition, they somehow already know what you truly want to become. Everything else is secondary." –**Steve Jobs**

"When one door closes, another opens; but we often look so long and so regretfully upon the closed door that we do not see the one which has opened for us." –**Alexander Graham Bell**

"Don't say you don't have enough time. You have exactly the same number of hours per day that were given to Helen Keller, Pasteur, Michelangelo, Mother Teresa, Leonardo da Vinci, Thomas Jefferson, and Albert Einstein." –**H. Jackson Brown Jr.**

"Our greatest weakness lies in giving up. The most certain way to succeed is always to try just one more time." – **Thomas A. Edison**

"If you don't go after what you want, you'll never have it. If you don't ask, the answer is always no. If you don't step forward, you're always in the same place." –**Nora Roberts**

“Believe in yourself and all that you are. Know that there is something inside you that is greater than any obstacle.” – **Christian D. Larson**

“There are far, far better things ahead than any we leave behind.” – **C.S. Lewis**

“Climbing to the top demands strength, whether it is to the top of Mount Everest or to the top of your career.” - **Abdul Kalam**

"The greatest discovery of my generation is that human beings can alter their lives by altering their attitudes of mind." - **William James**

"Whenever you're in conflict with someone, there is one factor that can make the difference between damaging your relationship and deepening it. That factor is attitude." - **William James**

“Happiness is an attitude. We either make ourselves miserable, or happy and strong. The amount of work is the same.” - **Francesca Reigler**

"Weakness of attitude becomes weakness of character!" - **Albert Einstein**

"Attitude is a little thing that makes a big difference." - **Winston Churchill**

"It's not what happens to you, but how you react to it that matters." - **Epictetus**

"Great minds can be found among young people around 20 years. They are full of imagination" – **Abdul Kalam**

"Keep your mind open to change all the time. Welcome it. Court it. It is only by examining and reexamining your opinions and ideas that you can progress."- **Dale Carnegie**

"Instead of worrying about what people say of you, why not spend time trying to accomplish something they will admire." - **Dale Carnegie**

"If you got it, ask yourself why and try to repeat the action. If you failed, ask yourself why and try to learn from the experience." - **Dale Carnegie**

"Learning is an active process. We learn by doing. Only knowledge that is used sticks in your mind." - **Dale Carnegie**

"The ideas I stand for are not mine. I borrowed them from Socrates. I swiped them from Chesterfield. I stole them from Jesus. And I put them in a book. If you don't like their rules, whose would you use?" - **Dale Carnegie**

"The only way to get the best of an argument is to avoid it." - **Dale Carnegie**

"When dealing with people, remember you are not dealing with creatures of logic, but creatures of emotion." - **Dale Carnegie**

"A teacher is a compass that activates the magnets of curiosity, knowledge, and wisdom in the pupils." - **Terri Guillemets**

"Change your thoughts and you change your world." — **Norman Vincent Peale**

"Having a second chance makes you want to work even harder."—**Tia Mowry**

"I believe that we are here for each other, not against each other. Everything comes from an understanding that you are a gift in my life—whoever you are, whatever our differences."—**John Denver**

"When we quit thinking primarily about ourselves and our own self-preservation, we undergo a truly heroic transformation of consciousness."—**Joseph Campbell**

"The minute a person whose word means a great deal to others dares to take the open-hearted and courageous way, many others follow."—**Marian Anderson**

"All that is valuable in human society depends upon the opportunity for development accorded individual."—Albert Einstein

"Opportunity is more powerful even than conquerors and prophets."—**Benjamin Disraeli**

"Move out of your comfort zone. You can only grow if you are willing to feel awkward and uncomfortable when you try something new."—**Brian Tracy**

"One of the beautiful things about baseball is that every once in a while you come into a situation where you want to, and where you have to, reach down and prove something."—**Nolan Ryan**

"All that we are is the result of what we have thought. The mind is everything. What we think we become."-**Gauthama Buddha.**

"The tree laden with fruits always bends low. If you wish to be great, be lowly and meek."– **Sri Ramakrishna Paramahamsa**

"You must be the change you want to see in the world." — **Mahatma Gandhi.**

"Failure comes only when we forget our ideals and objectives and principles." - **Jawaharlal Nehru**

"There is an important distinction between barriers to entry and barriers to imitation." - **C.K.Prahalad**

"God gives us dreams a size too big so that we can grow in them." – **Author Unknown**

"Your work is to discover your world and then with all your heart give yourself to it." – **Buddha**

"How you achieve results will shape the kind of person you become." – **C.K.Prahalad**

"Always aim at complete harmony of thought and word and deed. Always aim at purifying your thoughts and everything will be well." - Mahatma Gandhi

"As long as you derive inner help and comfort from anything, keep it." - **Mahatma Gandhi**

"The error of youth is to believe that intelligence is a substitute for experience, while the error of age is to believe experience is a substitute for intelligence." - **Ernest Hemingway**

"Freedom is not worth having if it does not include the freedom to make mistakes." - **Mahatma Gandhi**

"Happiness is when what you think, what you say, and what you do are in harmony."- **Mahatma Gandhi**

"It is unwise to be too sure of one's own wisdom. It is healthy to be reminded that the strongest might weaken and the wisest might err." - **Mahatma Gandhi**

"All that we are is the result of what we have thought. If a man speaks or acts with an evil thought, pain follows him. If a man speaks or acts with a pure thought, happiness follows him, like a shadow that never leaves him."- **Gauthama Buddha**

"An insincere and evil friend is more to be feared than a wild beast; a wild beast may wound your body, but an evil friend will wound your mind."- **Gauthama Buddha**

"Truth can be stated in a thousand different ways, yet each one can be true." - **Swami Vivekananda**

"You have to grow from the inside out. None can teach you, none can make you spiritual. There is no other teacher but your own soul." - **Swami Vivekananda**

"God, our Creator, has stored within our minds and personalities, great potential strength and ability. Prayer helps us tap and develop these powers."- **Abdul Kalam**

"Losers live in the past. Winners learn from the past and enjoy working in the present toward the future." - **Denis Waitley**

"If you have faith in all the three hundred and thirty millions of your mythological gods, … and still have no faith in yourselves, there is no salvation for you. Have faith in yourselves, and stand up on that faith and be strong; that is what we need." – **Swami Vivekananda**

"Study while others are sleeping; work while others are loafing; prepare while others are playing; and dream while others are wishing." - **William Arthur Ward**

"You can teach a student a lesson for a day; but if you can teach him to learn by creating curiosity, he will continue the learning process as long as he lives." - **Clay P. Bedford**

"Eklavya an ideal for modern students, Learnt archery without any external help." – **Swami Vivekananda**

"True leadership must be for the benefit of the followers not the enrichment of the leaders." - **Robert Townsend**

"You must have control of the authorship of your own destiny. The pen that writes your life story must be held in your own hand." - **Irene C. Kassorla**

"I never see what has been done; I only see what remains to be done." - **Gauthama Buddha**

"Hatred does not cease by hatred, but only by love; this is the eternal rule." - **Gauthama Buddha**

"Do what best you can do today thinking that there is no tomorrow. While learning think that you live longer and while sharing knowledge think that today is the last day in life. You will never be happy if you continue to search for what happiness consists of. You will never live if you are looking for the meaning of life." - **Albert Camus**

"Developing excellent communication skills is absolutely essential to effective leadership. The leader must be able to share knowledge and ideas to transmit a sense of urgency and enthusiasm to others. If a leader can't get a message across clearly and motivate others to act on it, then having a message doesn't even matter."— **Gilbert Amelio**

"Toughness gives you the resilience to keep pressing on, even if your determination and optimism are lagging." -- **Denis Waitley**

"I'm convinced that we can write and live our own scripts more than most people will acknowledge. I also know the price that must be paid. It's a real struggle to do it. It requires visualization and affirmation. It involves living a life of integrity, starting with making and keeping promises, until the whole human personality the senses, the thinking, the feeling, and the intuition are ultimately integrated and harmonized." - **Stephen R. Covey**

"What counts in life is not the mere fact that we have lived. It is what difference we have made to the lives of others that will determine the significance of the life we lead." **- Nelson Mandela, Former President of South Africa**

Dedication

Dedicated to Swami Vivekananda on the eve of his 150th birth anniversary - a youth icon and leader inspired millions of Indians.

To my students who travelled along with me in my life journey. The list is countless but here are a few of them who are the emerging young leaders – Tanveer Nigar, Ponugoti Sreeja, Bandaru Neelam, Mooga Sruthi, Mojjada Praveena, Lelapalli Naga Lakshmi, Kadiyam Sravani, J. Sushma Reddy, Gunjari Latha, Chilkuri Akhila, Meesala Sri Vidhya, Penmatsa Akhilasai Sneha, Ganji Sruthi, L. Prabhalika, Farha Nasreen, Farida Begum, Shakamuri Sirisha, M. Devika Rupa Anjali, Maddali Laxmi Swetha, Kalyan Katta, Goranthala Aravind Reddy, Ashish Barad, Kammara Ravi, Surasura Sukumar, and to my friends – Ginjupalli Sudha Rani, Narla Divya Uday, Bigulla Revathi, Magham Sri Ramachandra, Vankam Lokeswara Babu, Avvaru Venkata Kishore Babu, Potnuri Nagaraju, Yadla Kiran Kumar, Dhyapulai Nagendra Rao, Chavan Udaya Kiran, Zahoorullah S MD, Veesam Saibabu, Mannuru Vinay Kumar, and Chudumella Venkata Nageswawra Rao.

Foreword

Leadership begins inside of yourself, with discovering who you are and what you care about. But that's easier said than done, and doesn't necessarily come with age and experience. The earlier you can begin this process of self-exploration the better your chances are for facing the inevitable challenges and choices that life brings. Indeed, in a world of increasing complexity, turbulent marketplaces, where there is no place to hide from knowledge and difficult, if not impossible, to hide below the radar, it is crucial that you have an internal compass to guide and navigate your way into the future.

Professor M. S. Rao has provided his map of this terrain, the questions to ask yourself (and others), the proverbial ropes to know and the ropes to skip. He speaks plainly, even bluntly, about many of the important issues and choices you have to make, even while acknowledging that in the final analysis, no one can tell you what to do and the choice is always yours to make (making you responsible for the consequences). Of course, the choices are not always clear, seldom easy or convenient, but in the making of each one you build personal character, in the same sense that any home must be built upon a strong foundation with solid structural pillars or it won't be able to withstand either time or the vicissitudes of weather.

There are valuable lessons within these chapters, and you should visit them with an open heart and think about what speaks to you and your experiences. No need to either rush through this book, or your life. Starting the discernment process, and developing the ability to reflectively engage with the world, while you are a student is just one of the gifts offered in this book. Take advantage of this opportunity to liberate the leader within you.

Barry Z. Posner

Accolti Endowed Professor of Leadership

Leavey School of Business

Santa Clara University (USA)

Co-author: *The Leadership Challenge, Credibility*, and *The Truth About Leadership*

Preface

"We must do all that we can, to give our children the best in education and social upbringing - for while they are the youth of today, they shall be the leaders of tomorrow." - John F. Kennedy

Welcome to *Student Leaders: Growing From Students To CEOs.* You may be wondering why I am doing another book on leadership. I am an ardent follower of Swami Vivekananda and the year 2013 commemorates his 150th birth anniversary. As a tribute to this legend I authored this book on student leadership. This book grooms students as great leaders.

The book is divided into three Parts with Part I introducing student leadership; Part II unveiling 11 success sutras for students; and Part III inspiring students to grow as CEOs.

Part I begins with the ideas and ideals of Swami Vivekananda who inspired millions of Indian youth. It defines, explains and elaborates student leadership and describes campus leadership programs. It provides a blueprint to build leadership skills in students. It suggests the content plan for student leadership development program with training strategy. It explains the importance of building leadership skills to enhance employment opportunities in students. It advances an integrated approach and coordinated efforts from various stakeholders including educators, students, parents, educational institutions, industry and Non-Governmental Organizations (NGO) to enable students shift from campus to corporate as leaders successfully. It reminds that we need to dig tons of ore to get an ounce of gold. It declares that the future of any country depends on developing healthy minds in healthy bodies which is possible by cultivating a unique mindset, toolset and skills set in students. It illustrates introvert and extrovert leaders with a case study and unveils that leadership shift is possible from introversion to extroversion and vice versa.

Part II begins with an example of an eagle which is compared with a leader. It implores to grow like an eagle with a case study. It lists out the leaders who made things happen with their persistence when there seemed to be no light at the end of the tunnel. It elaborates the significance of transferable skills to fast-track your career. It explores the importance of time and unfurls 21 timeless tools to manage your time. It explains the significance of time, and elaborates with illustrations to manage your time. It enlightens that the biggest gift you can give to others is not money, but time. It cautions that if you waste one second, you wasted one second of your life as God gifted us a limited lifespan.

It lists out a few challenges the students encounter when they hit the corporate world. It prepares them to face corporate challenges squarely to come out with flying colors. It underscores the importance professional image and unveils the tools to build your professional image. It describes the usage of 'mirroring technique' to influence others and to win friends. It suggests blending hard and soft skills to scale senior positions quickly within the organization. It differentiates between hard and soft skills with a case study and connects them with left and right-brain respectively. It distinguishes between book smarts and street smarts. It highlights the changing mindset of Gen Y to work with smart leaders who treat them as partners rather than as subordinates; who are good at their technical expertise and are polite and pleasing in handling partners. It substantiates with examples of a wide range of leaders who failed due to dearth of soft skills and bounced back subsequently by blending hard and soft skills proportionately. It suggests the need for leaders to acquire soft skills along with hard skills to handle knowledge workers who crave for partnership rather than the traditional command-and-control managerial hierarchy and relationship.

It unrolls ideas and insights for change leaders to embrace change effectively. It equips them with tools and techniques to manage internal and external business environment to effect change successfully. It explains change, the importance of change, and change leadership. It outlines the causes of resistance, and unveils strategies to overcome them. It asserts that the only thing constant in the corporate world is change and competition. It calls upon change leaders to mould as per the changing business environment.

It advises and outlines tips to raise your bar constantly with the profile of Mary Kom who won the bronze medal in Boxing in the London Olympics 2012. It conveys the message of Lord Shri Krishna to emphasize on efforts, not on outcomes.

Part III begins with a cautious message that the industry looks for deployable students rather than employable students. It uncovers 21 timeless tools to become a CEO.

It provides a blueprint to touch your career tipping point quickly. It enlightens that leadership is a journey and enjoy your journey to become a CEO. It highlights some of the challenges encountered by HR leaders to excel as CEOs and presents the blueprint to help them achieve this. It emphasizes on the need to acquire CEO acumen and elaborates the importance of understanding other departments including marketing, finance, operations, legal, IT and strategy. It advises to close the gap between theory and practice. It stresses the importance of entering into line organizations rather than staff organizations for quick career advancement for HR leaders. It outlines a blueprint to coach future leaders by spotting the right talent. It implores to achieve success with integrity. It unfolds 12 steps to become a living legend. It concludes with an inspiring message to student leaders to develop a great attitude to keep India on the global map as a Super Power.

The book contains four Appendixes. Appendix A compares Obama with optimism and Lincoln with leadership as both hailed from humble origins. Appendix B unveils leadership lessons from Abraham Lincoln based on the film 'Lincoln' I saw. It helps readers learn lessons from Lincoln to become good leaders. Appendix C introduces 'Soft Leadership' coined by me, and it compares Mahatma Gandhi as a soft leader. Soft leadership is based on 11 characteristics - character, charisma, conscience, conviction, courage, communication, compassion, commitment, consistency, consideration, and contribution. Appendix D highlights the questions and answers about 'Soft Leadership'. I led a webinar as a thought leader titled, *Soft Leadership: A New Direction to Leadership* organized by world's prestigious International Leadership Association (ILA) which generated great interest with questions internationally. I have outlined the questions raised by participants with my answers for the benefit of readers.

I hope this book will inspire you to make it a priority, learn as much as you can on student leadership to excel as a successful leader and to reach CEO positions quickly.

Professor M.S.Rao

Acknowledgments

Writing a book is never a solo project. I am deeply indebted to many people whose expertise, wisdom, and encouragement kept me going. My wife's and children's (Ganesh Sai and Ramakrishna Sayee) encouragement and sacrifice made this book possible, and for that I am forever thankful. My wife, Padmavathy is a symbol of sacrifice and support for my books, and also is an immeasurable blessing in my life.

Several quotes, examples and anecdotes are the result of a collection from different sources. It is practically impossible to acknowledge each one of them separately. While I have tried to give credit wherever it is due, in case if I have missed anything, I will give due credit in future editions if it is brought to my notice.

I thank Dr. A.P.J. Abdul Kalam, former President of India from the core of my heart for permitting me to use his pledge in the penultimate chapter. I thank everyone including the team of Shroff Publishers & Distributors Pvt. Ltd. for publication of this book. I specifically thank Sunil Shastri, Marketing Manager of Shroff Publishers & Distributors Pvt. Ltd. for his initiative, positive attitude, and professionalism in publication of this book.

I express special thanks to all the readers who graciously took time off from their busy schedules to write to me, and share their views, and offer feedback on my books

21 Success Sutras for Leaders;
Smart Leadership: Lessons for Leaders;
Secrets of Your Leadership Success: The 11 Indispensable E's of a Leader;
Soft Leadership: Make Others Feel More Important;
Stand Out! Build a Successful Career and Become a Global Leader;
Sharpen Your Mind: Acquire Tools to Achieve Your Success;
Strategies for Improving Your Business Communication: The Book for Leaders to Communicate and Achieve Professional Success;
Sage Advice for Students and Educators: Stay Inspired!
Soup for Academic Leaders: Acquire Teaching Tools to Achieve Your Academic Leadership Success;
Spirit of Indian Youth: Soft Skills for Young Managers;
Smartness Guide: Success Tools for Students;
Spot Your Leadership Style: Build Your Leadership Brand;
Secrets for Success: Failure is only a Comma, Not a Full Stop;
Soft Skills: Enhancing Employability;
Soft Skills for Students: Classroom to Corporate
Success Sutras for Students: Stay Inspired!
and *Success Tools for Freshers: Soar Like Eagles!*

I wholeheartedly thank you for your endless support and love.

Contents

1

Swami Vivekananda – A Youth Leader

"Take up one idea. Make that one idea your life - think of it, dream of it; live on that idea. Let the brain, muscles, nerves, every part of your body, be full of that idea, and just leave every other idea alone. This is the way to success - that is the way great spiritual giants are produced." – Swami Vivekananda

Welcome to *Student Leaders: Growing From Students To CEOs.* I have authored this book to impart leadership skills in Indian students and groom them as leaders. India has a huge population and there is need for building leaders as per the size of population. However, we don't find adequate institutions and appropriate ambience to build leadership skills and abilities in Indian students. Most of the educational institutions don't provide campus leadership training programs to students. This book endeavors to create awareness about campus leadership training and student leadership and to fill the gap by providing right ideas, and insights to groom Indian students as leaders. I have a dream to see Indian students as good citizens. I have a vision to train and groom Indian students as great leaders. Hence, I have chosen the teaching profession as a career to accomplish my vision. And I am excited to see this book in your hands!

I am passionate about Indian students and youth. I play an instrumental role to shape Indian students as great leaders. I am an ardent follower of Swami Vivekananda who was a symbol of youth power and a youth icon. I have authored this book exclusively for Swami Vivekananda on the eve of his 150th birth anniversary as a tribute to this leadership legend. Therefore, I would like to begin this book with his ideas and ideals.

1863 2013

150th

Birth anniversary of

Swami Vivekananda

आत्मनो मोक्षार्थं जगद्धिताय च

Swami Vivekananda's Ideas and Ideals

In March 2013, I attended a seminar on Swami Vivekananda to find out the latest developments and to know how his messages are spread across the country. His birth anniversary is celebrated as National Youth Day in India as a mark of respect to this youth legend. I read books about him 25 years ago and acquired lots of knowledge and share it with my students regularly.

Swami Vivekananda is known to every Indian, and most of the Indian youth follow his footsteps. His initial name was Narendra Nath Datta. He was born in an affluent family in Kolkata on 12 January 1863. His father, Vishwanath Datta, was a successful attorney with interests in a wide range of subjects, and his mother, Bhuvaneshwari Devi. He was a symbol of true spiritualism, secularism and modernism. He was the first leader to walk the whole of India to connect with masses and inspire youth. Probably he was the first Indian leader to address the audience as the brothers and sisters of the world. He was the link between the past and present and bridge between the west and the east.

Swami Vivekananda implored Indian youth to possess 'muscles of iron' and 'nerves of steel' to make India a great country in the world. He was the proud son of India who awakened great interest about India and Indians globally. He was a powerful orator whose address at the World Parliament of Religions in Chicago catapulted him to fame in the US and attracted many Americans and Europeans to Indian spiritual traditions. He conquered America without any bullet through his preaching in the Chicago Conference. He voiced Vedanta as a vision for the spiritual regeneration of India that was fighting for independence from the British Empire.

Swami Vivekananda believed in character building among the Indian youth. He preached to Indians to be original and implored them to enhance concentration to achieve great success. He emphasized not only on good Indians but also on strong Indians who can preserve Indian civilization and values forever.

Currently the Indian youth are enamored by western culture and technology and it is time for them to change their mindset. It is unfortunate that they believe more in 'cell-confidence' rather than 'self-confidence'. They must emphasize on inspiration, intuition and innovation to grow India as a strong nation. They must respect and love our culture and at the same time they must take the best from the western culture as all cultures have unique features to understand, emulate and absorb.

The Indian youth are ambitious and hard working. They have lots of fire and passion but they lack the right direction and guidance. They are carried away by negativity rather than positivity. Hence, they need leadership educators who can handhold, guide and groom them as great leaders.

As you love your mother you must love your motherland. As you love your own brothers and sisters you must love all Indian citizens as brothers and sisters. It is time for the Indian youth to take up the challenge and lead from the front to make an economically vibrant India.

The future of India is in your hands. Swami Vivekananda dedicated his entire life to religious tolerance and universal brotherhood. He emphasized on values among the Indian youth and, as a result, he is remembered forever as a youth leader. He is a legend who lived beyond his times and continues to live forever in the history of India. The present youth must understand his ideas; appreciate his ideals; and apply his principles and philosophies to create a vibrant and great India.

India is the world's most youthful nation. We need not only youth leaders but also youth-led leaders. When you awaken the youth you awaken India. Therefore, all stakeholders including educators, parents, elders and NGOs must guide the youth in the right direction to prepare them as good and strong citizens and leaders so that they lead this nation with confidence to make India a Super Power.

"Arise, Awake and Stop not until the goal is reached" – Swami Vivekananda.

Pledge: Believe in fraternity and universal brotherhood.

I Have a Dream

I have a dream that one day the Indian youth will spread across the world and they will be in great demand globally. I have a dream that the Indian youth will become more responsible with a great attitude to take on the global challenges.

I have a dream that the Indian youth will bring back our past glory by putting India on the top of the world.

I have a dream that we Indians will work and walk as brothers and sisters.

I have a dream that we Indians will look at the commonalities, not the differences.

I have a dream that we Indians will stay united and become role model for other citizens in the world.

I have a dream that the sun will not set on Indians.

I have a dream that the Indian youth will lead this country from the front and make it a Super Power in the world.

God bless India! Jai Hind!

References

http://speakermix.com/professor-m-s-rao

http://www.facebook.com/pages/Professor-MSRao/451516514937414?skip_nax_wizard=true

Author's Blogs:

http://professormsraoguru.blogspot.com

http://professormsrao.blogspot.com

http://profmsr.blogspot.com

2

Student Leadership

"I would caution student teachers to always be flexible with kids, but not to leave them with no structure, because many times we are the only structure these kids have." - Jim Kouzes and Barry Posner

To build great leaders, it is essential to build leadership skills early among the youth. It is advisable to hone leadership skills among students as it is the right age to mould and groom them as leaders. It is for this reason, military takes young people and trains them as leaders. The success rate of military leaders is higher than the civilian leaders because of rigorous training imparted at a tender age. In this chapter we will discuss student leadership, its importance and campus leadership programs to groom students as leaders. But before you learn them, you must understand yourself first to lead others.

Understand Yourself First to Lead Others

Lao Tzu quoted, "If you understand others you are smart. If you understand yourself you are illuminated. If you overcome others you are powerful. If you overcome yourself you have strength. If you know how to be satisfied you are rich. If you can act with vigor, you have a will. If you don't lose your objectives you can be long-lasting."

Understanding yourself is a great asset to excel as a leader. But a few people are aware of themselves and the majority have the attitude of judging others. We will discuss about self-awareness which is a major tool to develop students as leaders.

People who are aware of themselves are realistic as they know their strengths and weaknesses accurately and achieve whatever they want in life. They neither underestimate nor overestimate themselves. They can lead effectively as they understand themselves and also their team members. If they make mistakes they realize quickly as they are aware of their weaknesses and move forward by learning lessons.

Ken Blanchard once remarked, "Feedback is the breakfast of champions." Hence, take feedback from others constantly to understand yourself. Don't defend yourself when others give you feedback. Listen to them carefully and accept it gracefully without any false prestige. Thank the feedback givers for their time and concern. Subsequently go to a serene place and reflect on the received feedback. Find out the areas where you have limitations and overcome with practice. Remember that nobody is free from weaknesses.

Leaders judge others a lot but they must know about themselves first to achieve leadership effectiveness. Being aware of yourself helps you guard from your weaknesses and capitalize on your strengths. It helps in forming great teams to execute tasks effectively. Before motivating others leaders must identify what motivates them. It makes things easier for leaders and achieves leadership effectiveness quickly thus accomplishing the organizational objectives. Writing articles improves your thinking skills. You will be able to analyze and understand yourself. This is one of the techniques to discover yourself.

If you want to be honest with others you have to be honest with yourself first. When you want to assess others you must assess yourself first. When you judge the strengths and weaknesses of others you must judge your own strengths and weaknesses. Remember, the people who understand others are wise and those who understand themselves are enlightened. Stephen R. Covey rightly remarked, "Every human has four endowments- self awareness, conscience, independent will and creative imagination. These give us the ultimate human freedom... The power to choose, to respond, to change."

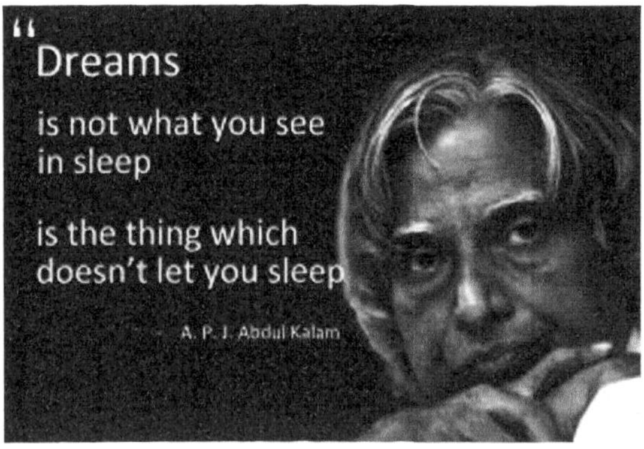

What is Student Leadership?

Student leadership is the process of setting a vision, making decisions, building teams, motivating others, and aligning their energies and efforts to accomplish the collective objectives and goals. This leadership helps students excel as successful leaders in future irrespective of the area of interest and industry they are into. It prepares students to face challenges squarely to come out with flying colors. With the rapid growth in technologies there is growing volatility, uncertainty, complexity and ambiguity everywhere. Hence, preparing students within the campus or educational institutions helps them grow quickly in their lives.

Student Leadership – Importance

Jack Zenger unveils the research findings in his article entitled, '*Start LD Early When is the Right Time?*' in Leadership Excellence, April 2013 as follows: "We examined data on 17,000 leaders to learn their age when they participated in their company's Leadership Development (LD) process. We discovered that the average age was 42. Less than 5 percent were under

27, only 10 percent under 30. On average, supervisors would wait nine years before participating in any LD program!"

Jack Zenger says, starting LD earlier has five benefits: They are: Easier to learn new principles and to practice them correctly at a younger age; avoid acquiring bad habits; longer time to practice; the organization benefits from improved skills; and the longer we wait, the less success we're likely to have. Hence, it is essential to start the LD process early and especially within the campus to prepare students to face challenges with confidence in the later part of their lives.

Campus Leadership Programs

"Ideal teachers are those who use themselves as bridges over which they invite their students to cross, then having facilitated their crossing, joyfully collapse, encouraging them to create bridges of their own." - Nikos Kazantzakis

While designing Leadership Development Program (LDP) course curriculum for students it is essential to keep short-term and long-term goals in view. The leadership educators must look at what is immediately required for students and also what is required in future for their growth. They must adopt the following steps to build leadership skills in students within the campus:

1. Build confidence in students that leadership skills can be acquired by sharing anecdotes, examples, illustrations and striking stories.
2. Engage students to work in an organization as academics teach the science of thinking, but experience teaches the art—the street smarts.
3. Encourage them to participate in sports, games, club activities and NGO activities.
4. Send them for military training on voluntary basis for a brief time to groom them as leaders because the military is the best ground for learning real leadership skills for students. It not only builds patriotism but also builds

discipline and leadership skills which are very essential for students.

5. Promote Emotional Quotient (EQ) among students. Emphasize on dialogue skills and listening skills within the campus to enhance employability and capture the prevailing opportunities globally.
6. Encourage students to write as it clears the clutter from their minds and provides clarity. It helps in self-reflection, and self-discovery leading to self-awareness.
7. Implore them to learn from their own mistakes and from others' mistakes and it serves as a productive self-development tool. Remember, nobody can become a crackshot unless they lose some ammunition.
8. Align their aptitude and energies as per the curriculum.
9. Above all, build integrity among students which is a very challenging task for educators. Psychologist Patricia King rightly remarked, "Helping students develop the integrity and strength of character that prepare them for

> leadership may be one of the most challenging and important goals of higher education."

Currently organizations are focusing their LDPs on Gen X (born from 1955 to 1976). Instead they must focus on Gen Y (born from 1977 to 1998) who will be more productive and useful in the long run. Training and grooming them enhances employee engagement and loyalty. It enhances productivity and performance in the workplace. Overall, it improves the organizational bottom lines. In addition, trained people can be kept in the leadership pipeline to avert any organization eventuality which may arise due to sudden resignation of senior leaders. To go further, it is advisable to set a vision and create a voice to groom students as leaders within the educational institution itself to enable them to shift from campus to corporate with confidence.

"A good student is someone who listens to what I say, adapting my teachings to his life, but never following it literally. It is someone who doesn't look for a job, but looks for work that dignifies him. And lastly, it isn't someone who seeks to be noticed, but someone who seeks to make something notable." – Confucius

Pledge: Start leadership development process early in the students.

Reference

Start LD Early When is the Right Time? by Jack Zenger, Leadership Excellence April, 2013

3

A Blueprint to Build Student Leaders

"If your actions inspire others to dream more, learn more, do more and become more, you are a leader." - John Quincy Adams

There are mushrooming leadership development programs for students in the developed countries to build leadership skills and abilities in students. Some prestigious international universities including Harvard Business School have customized training programs offering courses and degrees in the domain of leadership. However, there are no such initiatives in India despite being the second largest populated country in the world with the highest number of youth. In fact, there is a huge potential for student leadership training programs in India. Unfortunately, there are no structured and organized methods to impart leadership training for students in India except in a few premier business schools.

Leaders are Made, not Born

During my leadership training programs I often come across students raising questions whether leaders are born or made. I try hard to persuade them that leaders are made rather than born. Most of the leadership depends on emotional intelligence that can be cultivated through teaching, training, observation, experience and practice. Hence, anybody can acquire leadership qualities unlike talents which are inborn, and the same has been substantiated by a number of international leadership gurus including Warren Bennis, Stephen R. Covey, Ken Blanchard and John Maxwell.

Enhances Employment Opportunities for Students

Most companies look for leadership skills among their employees. First, it is the attitude that creates a great impression and connects with the HR during the employment interview. Secondly, it is the leadership skills that tip the scale in favor of the selection. Hence, it is essential for students to acquire leadership skills in the educational institutions to enable them to demonstrate during interviews to grab employment offers. Leadership helps them lead their lives with confidence and mettle. They can survive in any part of the world. Hence, it is strongly recommended to encourage and build leadership skills in students.

LDP for Students

Developing leadership skills in students needs an integrated approach and coordinated efforts from various stakeholders including educators, students, parents, educational institutions, industry and Non Governmental Organizations (NGO) to enable students shift from campus to corporate as leaders successfully.

There is need for innovative leadership development programs for students as the days of traditional training of 'command and control' don't work any longer. Keeping the current volatility, increased uncertainty, complexity and ambiguity in view, the content has to be crafted and customized accordingly to meet the current needs. Although the list of topics to be included in the student leadership training program is lengthy here are some of the key topics to be covered during the training program:

- Student Leadership: Define student leadership, and explain why it is needed to build leaders for tomorrow. Share various leadership styles including situational leadership style. Provide examples of some students leaders globally who made a profound impact on students.
- Communication Skills: Communication is the sister of leadership. It is essential to improve communication skills in students so that they can articulate their vision, ideas and insights effectively.
- Emotional Intelligence. Emotional intelligence is a key ingredient of leadership and Daniel Goleman highlighted its importance. Emotional Intelligence Quotient (EQ) is much superior to the so-called Intelligence Quotient (IQ). Students must learn how to work in team dynamics to enhance their EQ. In addition, EQ is much needed in the current complex world to help work in stressful conditions.
- Team Building: Practice is one of the best ways to build leadership skills and abilities. It is possible when students work in teams. Ken Blanchard once remarked, "None of us is as smart as all of us." Hence, encourage students to participate in

team activities as team building is the brother of leadership.

- Decision Making Skills: Students must know how to make decisions by blending their head, heart and gut. Most of them think that all the decisions they make must go right. But in reality very few decisions will deliver positive outcomes. They must learn lessons from failures and move forward with confidence.
- Public Speaking Skills: Encourage students to deliver speeches in the presence of other students. It builds their confidence, and they will be able to inspire others.
- Feedback: Provide feedback immediately to the students as it helps students recognize their blind spots and overcome them successfully.
- Activities: Organize more of activities such as cross country training, jungle training, simulated united national assembly, mountaineering, and river rafting to name a few.

It is rightly said, "People forget how fast you did a job-but they remember how well you did it. The price of greatness is responsibility. We are continually faced by great opportunities brilliantly disguised as insoluble problems.

Every job is a self-portrait of the person who did it. Autograph your work with excellence." Hence, teach students to emphasize on excellence as it makes a huge difference in their lives apart from growing as effective leaders. Precisely, design and deliver students leadership development programs in such a way that students develop a unique mindset, toolset, skill set to grow as leaders in the long run.

Training Methodology

It is ideal to have 15 students in each training session to enhance its effectiveness. The training methodology must be as follows: 40 percent of the training must be talking time with concepts, case studies, examples, illustrations, and striking stories of successful international student leaders. Case study discussion helps students not only to express their ideas clearly in groups but also to appreciate others' viewpoints. It enhances their creativity, decision making and trouble shooting skills. Above all, it helps them think through out-of-the box to come out with innovative solutions. 50 percent of the time must be allocated on experiential learning such as role-plays, team activities and exercises. Encourage students to think through critically by shooting them with hypothetical questions. The remaining 10 percent of the training time must be allocated for giving feedback to students to assess whether they improved their leadership behavior and ensured effective takeaways.

Blueprint to Build Student Leaders

Role of Students: Learning leadership is like learning how to swim. Only when you get into water you learn the art of swimming. Hence, take the plunge to lead from the front to soar like an eagle. Here are some of the ways to acquire leadership skills and abilities:

- Be passionate to lead from the front with a heart to make a difference in the lives of others.
- Visualize yourself as a leader as visualization is one of the effective tools to achieve whatever you want in your life. Remember, a battle is won twice – first in the mind and second in real life.
- Apply the SWOT tool to assess your strengths and weaknesses, and search for opportunities from threats.
- Work in teams to understand team dynamics and improve your emotional intelligence. Practice is the most effective way to learn any skill and

leadership is not an exception. You cannot become a crackshot unless you lose some ammunition.

- Join a toastmasters' club or local leadership associations to network and grab opportunities to participate and deliver speeches.
- Be a risk taker. Avoid the fear of failure or criticism as failures are part of life and criticism helps you improve.
- Hire a coach who helps you build skills and abilities apart from bringing out behavioral improvements to become a leader.
- Take successful leaders as your role model. Find out the qualities you admire and acquire them.
- Read inspirational books. Most of the leaders are great readers including Abraham Lincoln.
- Find out the problems that affect the people; create a common cause; influence the people; build a strong team; align their energies and efforts; and motivate them constantly to accomplish your goals and objectives.
- Delegate routine tasks to others so that you can find more time to undertake higher challenging roles and responsibilities.

- Spread the fame when things go well and take the blame when things go wrong.
- Learn, unlearn and relearn as the world is changing rapidly. In addition, what works now might not work in future due to increased uncertainty, volatility, complexity and ambiguity everywhere.

Role of Educators: Educators must take the initiative to build leadership skills in students to enable students to find themselves comfortable to lead in the corporate world. For instance, they must encourage students to participate in simulated 'United Nations Assembly' which is a mock exercise for students wherein students represent various countries in the world and discuss and debate on pressing global issues. Students can also discuss the ways and means to ensure global peace and security and maintain ecological balance. Educators must also encourage students to participate in group discussions and debates to develop leadership skills.

Role of Education Institutions: Education institutions must do the following activities:

- Organize events, functions, conferences, tours and excursions. Also, conduct industry visits for students to expose them to the practical world to build skills.
- Nominate a class representative for each classroom to build coordination and leadership skills.
- Encourage students to participate in NCC, NSS, and NGO where they work with other team members; they are the right avenues to learn team dynamics to build leadership skills.
- Teach them how to handle pressure; work under stress; and manage increased uncertainty to achieve all-round success in this century.
- Balance both curricular and extracurricular activities as presently Indian education institutions don't emphasize much on extracurricular activities. Building leadership skills falls in the bracket of extracurricular activities and these skills groom students as well-rounded personalities.

It is essential to build leaders on a continuous basis as the Baby Boomers are retiring and Gen X is unprepared to assume leadership roles and responsibilities resulting in a dearth of leadership talent in the leadership pipeline globally. In addition, the current complexity calls for leaders who can take on challenges head-on globally. Hence, it is essential to spot students with the X factor to groom them as leaders. If we want the society and civilization to survive and succeed we must address the issue of developing leaders globally especially among the youth. Hence, it is strongly recommended to include a course on leadership development along with soft skills to groom leaders for tomorrow.

Remember, we need to dig tons of ore to get an ounce of gold. It is applicable especially for building leaders. Everybody cannot grow as a leader. The people who are prepared to struggle and sacrifice can alone grow as leaders. The people who are ready to undergo trials and tribulations can only grow as successful leaders. Hence, students must realize that becoming a leader is not a cakewalk as the road is replete with several hurdles. When we observe Abraham Lincoln, he underwent lots of challenges in his lifetime; swallowed insults and finally, became President of America. He sacrificed his life to abolish slavery and end Civil War in America.

Conclusion

The future of any country depends on developing healthy minds in healthy bodies which is possible by cultivating a unique mindset, toolset and skills set in students. India has a few leaders when compared with the size of its population. Small countries produced the best leaders. What is wrong with India? Why is India unable to produce the best leaders in the world? India had a great leader like Swami Vivekananda who left an indelible mark internationally by spreading tolerance and universal brotherhood. India needs more such Vivekanandas to inspire the Indian youth to change their mindset with a proactive and positive attitude to make India on par with other advanced and civilized countries in the world.

"Do not follow where the path may lead. Go instead where there is no path and leave a trail." - Muriel Strode – Author

Pledge: Cultivate a unique mindset, toolset and skills set in students.

4

Introvert versus Extrovert Leaders

"The art of being yourself at your best is the art of unfolding your personality into the man you want to be. Be gentle with yourself, learn to love yourself, to forgive yourself, for only as we have the right attitude toward ourselves can we have the right attitude toward others." - Wilfred Peterson

Are you worried about being an introvert or an extrovert personality? Are you concerned that you are unable to communicate with others at ease being an introvert? Are you concerned that you are branded as a talkative person by others for being an extrovert? Do you think that you cannot convert from being an introvert to extrovert or vice versa? In fact, introversion or extroversion depends on the personality types coined by Myers and Briggs Type Indicator (MBTI) based on Carl Jung's theory of psychology. It outlines that there are 16 personality types in the world, and all are unique with their strengths and weaknesses.

Studies have shown that about one third to one half of the population consider themselves to be introverts and some of the successful people in the world are introverts by nature. Introverts often communicate less with others in the workplace and do their tasks silently. They are reserved by nature, stay aloof and keep away from publicity. Since they prefer to work alone they must choose careers such as research and consultancy to enjoy their work and contribute their best. In contrast, extroverts communicate more than an average individual. They are expressive by nature and appreciate working in teams. They must choose careers such as marketing and anchoring to enjoy their work and grow rapidly. There are people who shift from introversion to extroversion and vice versa as per the situation with ease. They are known as ambiverts. They are flexible, adaptable and situational and can lead others effectively. Ambiverts are good at emotional intelligence, and are tactful in managing and motivating the emotions, egos and feelings of others. Hence, they can prove to be effective leaders. It is observed that introverts often undersell while the extroverts often oversell. In fact, it is the ambiverts who sell themselves appropriately.

Case Study of Ron and Susan

Ron and Susan worked in an academic institution as professors where Ron was an introvert and Susan was an extrovert by nature. Ron performed his tasks silently without hogging the limelight and made significant academic achievements much bigger than Susan. In contrast, Susan achieved too little but blew her own trumpet with her colleagues and the owners of the educational institution. She presented papers for national and international seminars and exaggerated about her achievements to earn attention. The colleagues were vexed with her excessive talk and branded her as a chatter-box. Ron was silent by nature and did his own work and authored around 25 books but seldom talked about them as he preferred to be simple and humble.

Susan had the habit of showing her paper publications to the owners of the education institutions, and as a result, the owners had very high expectations from her. But Susan's colleagues approached the owners and complained about Susan and her attitude to downplay others and overplay her achievements. They also informed the owners that Ron was highly capable but rarely craved for public attention and recognition. Becoming fed up with

Susan's dominant and insulting behavior, half of the faculty members resigned from the educational institution. Finally, the owners realized that Susan was a chatterbox and became a liability rather than an asset to the institution. They asked Susan to leave the organization and requested the introvert Ron to lead the institution.

It is obvious from this story that being excessively extroverted dents the image of the individual and causes damage to the institution. In contrast, introverts may not get immediate attention and recognition but earn lasting respect from others. They command great respect from others for their simplicity and humility.

Leadership and Personality Types

In fact, leadership has nothing to do with introversion or extroversion. What matters at the end of the day is how leaders lead the team by persuading the people. If leaders are expert communicators they can easily persuade and achieve the organizational objectives. In this case, being an extrovert pays a lot for leaders. If leaders are not expert communicators, they may be good strategists and design a great blueprint to enable the people to follow and achieve organizational objectives. In this case, being an introvert pays a lot for leaders. It is obvious that both introversion and extroversion have their strengths and weaknesses. Hence, leaders can capitalize their strengths and lead from the front. Here goes the difference between introvert and extrovert leaders:

Introvert versus Extrovert Leaders

Introvert leaders are cool and composed. They reflect a lot and take intrapersonal feedback. They make decisions based on their head rather than on their heart and gut. Their success rate is higher but they find it tough to persuade others. In contrast, extrovert leaders are emotional and have the fear of losing their popularity and prestige. They take interpersonal feedback and may find less time for reflection. Hence, they may go more by heart rather than by head and gut. It is observed that introvert leaders are good listeners while extrovert leaders are good speakers. Introverts prefer to do background operations while extroverts prefer to do frontend operations. In a nutshell, introvert leaders are quiet leaders while extrovert leaders are noise leaders. Introverts can be compared with scholars while extroverts can be compared with practitioners and both are needed to achieve academic excellence.

A Study reveals that introvert leaders can handle proactive people while extrovert leaders can handle passive people effectively. Extrovert leaders often crave for popularity and fear to making tough decisions. In contrast, introvert leaders don't worry much about popularity and can make tough decisions. In addition, introverts are internally motivated and do not expect appreciation and encouragement from others. In contrast, extroverts are externally motivated and depend on others' appreciation and encouragement. Some of the successful introverts include Abraham Lincoln, Albert Einstein, Rosa Parks, Jeff Immelt and Bill Gates while some of the successful extroverts include Winston Churchill, John F. Kennedy, Martin Luther King, Jr., and Jack Welch.

Is a Leadership Shift Possible?

The Chinese philosopher, Lao-Tzu quoted, "Every human being's essential nature is perfect and faultless, but after years of immersion in the world we easily forget our roots and take on a counterfeit nature." Therefore, the shift from extroversion to introversion and vice versa is possible. The personalities can change as per age and experience. As experience is the best teacher, people change their personalities as per the situation. In order to shift, you must identify and understand your personality style and mould as per the situation. If you are in a leadership position you have to be proactive to shift from one type to another to achieve your organizational goals and objectives. Hence, discover your personality type; manage your personality; discover the personalities of the people around you; motivate and manage their personalities to achieve leadership success and effectiveness and to excel as an effective leader. To conclude, leaders must identify their employees based on personality types and apply different strokes to different personalities to achieve organizational excellence and effectiveness.

"Personality can open doors, but only character can keep them open." - Elmer G. Letterman

Pledge: Assess your personality type to explore leadership opportunities.

5

Grow Like an Eagle to Excel as an Effective Leader

"Opposition is a natural part of life. Just as we develop our physical muscles through overcoming opposition – such as lifting weights – we develop our character muscles by overcoming challenges and adversity." – Stephen R. Covey

The caption sounds strange for many readers. In fact, eagle is one of the rarest birds with unique characteristics. Before we understand about the eagle it is vital to discuss about relationships and goals.

When you look at a turtle it has low goals and relationships; a teddy bear has low goals but high relationships; a shark has high goals but low relationships; and a fox has medium goals and relationships. But it is the eagle which alone has high goals and relationships. In fact, the eagle is an exceptional bird with unique characteristics and qualities that stand out from others. It is often compared with a leader. Here goes the life story of an eagle:

When the eagle was in the egg, the mother eagle scratches the egg and the eagle is born with a lot of pain. The mother eagle teaches the challenges in life to the baby eagle and trains it the hard way. The mother eagle drops the baby eagle from the cliff to enable the latter to come out of its comfort zone and learn to fly. The mother eagle observes and ensures the safety of the baby eagle by not letting it fall on the ground and die. However, most times, the baby eagle develops strong wings by not falling on the ground as it struggles to fly, and finally, learns to fly sky high.

An eagle prepares for several challenges and overcomes them successfully during its lifetime. Whenever there is a thunderstorm most of the birds run for shelter and safety. But an eagle makes use of the thunderstorm and flies high as it knows how to convert threats into opportunities.

An eagle can see objects up to a distance of 5 kilometers. That is why an eagle is known as visionary. It is highly focused on its prey and eats fresh meat only. It doesn't eat stale meat. It wants the best in its life and does not compromise. When a female eagle wants to mate with a male eagle, it goes to a great height and drops a small stick from the sky. The female eagle appreciates the male eagle that goes fast and catches the stick before it hits the ground and gives back to it. Only then does the female eagle mate with the male eagle. Above all, an eagle reinvents from time to time and adapts to change quickly during its lifetime.

A Tale of Learning Swimming in a Hard Way

My two sons Ganesh and Ramu and I used to go for swimming when they were 7 and 5 years old respectively. I wanted to teach them swimming. My elder son, Ganesh was bold and a risk taker. Hence, he jumped into the water and somehow struggled and learned swimming. I observed him closely to ensure that he did not drown inside the water. That is how he learned swimming the hard way. However, my younger son, Ramu was scared of water, and he refused to get into the water to learn swimming. I persuaded him a number of times to get into the water and learn slowly. He did not follow my advice as he had fear of water. Then I lifted him physically and threw him into the water. He started to struggle, and finally came out of the water successfully. He yelled at me for throwing him inside the water and complained to my wife. My wife did not appreciate my act. I told my wife that we have to learn lessons in life the hard way to get the best out of us. Somehow I persuaded Ramu that I will not throw him into the water next time and implored him to come to the swimming pool to learn swimming. He came to the swimming pool after my several requests and assurances that I would not repeat such an act, and finally he acquired the art of swimming. He participated in swimming competition and earned a medal. From this experience, it becomes obvious that children must learn the hard way so that they can face challenges squarely and succeed in their lives ultimately.

Parents must prepare their children to face challenges in their lives. Giving wealth to children by parents may not be of much use in the present circumstances. What parents must realize is to provide good character and education to their children so that children can live in any part of the world successfully. Above all, parents must prepare their children to face all challenges so that children can excel as effective leaders and soar like eagles.

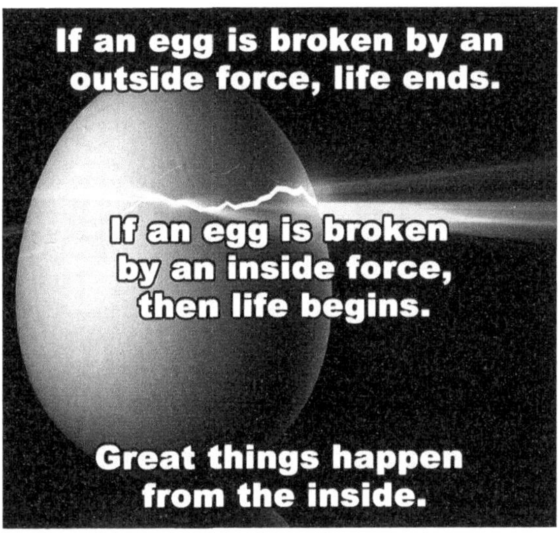

"Don't quack like a duck, soar like an eagle." - Ken Blanchard

Pledge: Come out of your comfort zone to soar like an eagle.

6

Make It Happen

"Nothing in the world can take the place of persistence.
Talent will not; nothing is more common than unsuccessful men with talent.
Genius will not; unrewarded genius is almost a proverb.
Education will not; the world is full of educated derelicts.
Persistence and determination alone are omnipotent.
The slogan "press on" has solved and always will solve the problems of the human race." - Calvin Coolidge

One of the major factors that differentiates between successful and unsuccessful people is persistence. Research has shown that only 3 percent of the people succeed while the rest remain as average or unsuccessful people. It is basically because the 3 percent people come out of their comfort zones and enter into effective zones. They make things happen. They persist when the entire world gives up. They know that it is often the last key in the bunch that would open the key. Hence, in this chapter we will discuss about the scientists, thinkers, entrepreneurs and leaders who made things happen when odds were stacked against them and when there was stiff opposition from all quarters and ridicule from others.

Thomas Alva Edison is an amazing example of a scientist who faced tons of failures and made things happen with his persistence. He failed 1000 times to invent the light bulb and ultimately succeeded. When asked about his failures he said they were not failures but the ways that didn't work to invent the bulb. Similarly, Alexander Graham Bell encountered a number of challenges while inventing the telephone and finally, made it happen in 1876.

A. P.J. Abdul Kalam rose from humble origins in a small village. He sold newspapers to earn his livelihood. He scripted the Space Odyssey of India. He had a number of failures as a scientist initially. He built the first rocket that crashed, and a missile that crashed. Everyone ridiculed him. But he did not give up. He persisted and succeeded as the Missile Man of India winning many awards including India's highest civilian award – the Bharat Ratna and finally, occupying the highest position as the President of India.

Columbus with his band of followers persisted to discover the sea route to America. Everyone said that it was impossible. But he endured the adversities, motivated his followers and finally discovered the sea route.

Michelangelo had strong visualization powers and discovered a stone and finally created one of the world's masterpieces – David. His persistence, vision and *'I can make it happen'* attitude helped achieve his goal.

The Wright brothers (Orville and Wilbur) were ridiculed when they tried to invent the airplane. They said, "We have a dream, and we can make it happen." They achieved their dream goal ultimately with tons of trials and tribulations and unsuccessful endeavors initially.

The famous Brooklyn Bridge connecting Manhattan Island to Brooklyn on the river was built by a creative engineer, John Roebling and his son Washington. Both had a great vision and a strong dream to build the bridge. Everyone ridiculed and said, "It is impossible. You crazy people cannot build it." Both father and son were confident and conceived a blueprint and worked on it. But a tragic accident took the life of John Roebling and injured his son, Washington who was bedridden and was not in a position to walk and talk. Everyone thought that the project would be shelved. But Washington developed a code to communicate his ideas and instructed through his fingers on the bed resulting in successful completion of the Brooklyn Bridge.

Colonel Sanders founded KFC in his old age with lots of initial failures. His recipe was rejected initially and ridiculed by many but he did not give up. He persisted and succeeded finally.

All these leaders made things happen when there seemed to be no light at the end of the tunnel. They did not let things happen, but made things happen with their passion, persistence and vision.

Develop 'I Can Make It Happen' Mindset

W.J. Davison quoted, "The life that conquers is the life that moves with a steady resolution and persistence toward a predetermined goal. Those who succeed are those who have thoroughly learned the immense importance of plan in life, and the tragic brevity of time." A battle is won twice – first in the mind and then in reality. Hence, firm up your thoughts with positive commands such as *'I can do it' and 'I can make it happen'.* Over a period of time, your behavior will change and actions will follow accordingly. You will remove 'can't' from your mind and replace it with 'can'. You believe in yourself. To achieve that status, give positive commands to your subconscious mind half an hour before you go to bed and they get reinforced in your subconscious mind and you dream accordingly. You speak positive and create a positive circle around you. You build a team of people with your vision and values and voice regularly to accomplish them. Here is the process to make it happen:

Create a blueprint keeping the end in mind. Stay clearly focused and build resources. Practice what you want to achieve through test runs. Manage distractions. Take feedback and align yourself from time to time through corrective steps and you will find yourself making things happen one day and standing out from others.

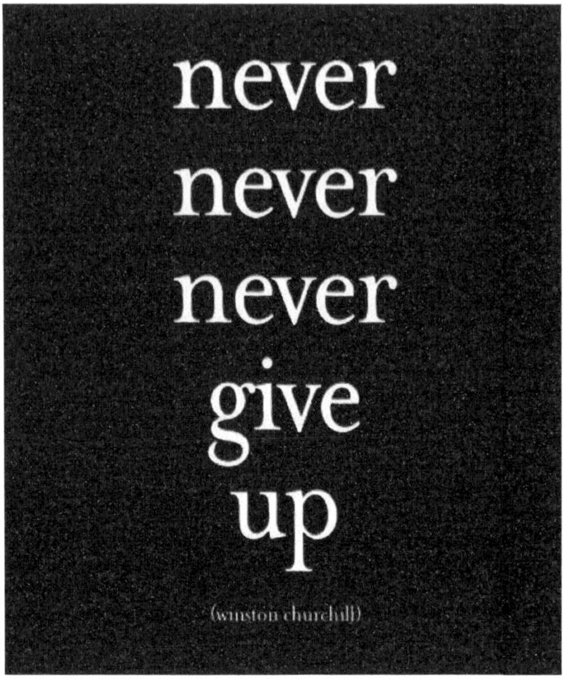

Conclusion

Swami Vivekananda once remarked, "It is our mental attitude which makes the world what it is for us. The whole world is in our minds." Hence, if you want to succeed you must have a broad vision and work on it relentlessly with a positive attitude and persistence. You will come out with flying colors one day. The entire world will applaud your achievements and you forget the pain you took to make things happen with others' recognition and appreciation. To conclude with the words of

Confucius, “Our greatest glory is not in never falling, but in rising every time we fall.”

"Failure is only postponed success as long as courage coaches ambition. The habit of persistence is the habit of victory." - Herbert Kaufman

Pledge: Develop the ‘I can make it happen’ mindset.

7

Acquire "Transferable Skills"

"Take advantage of every opportunity to practice your communication skills so that when important occasions arise, you will have the gift, the style, the sharpness, the clarity, and the emotions to affect other people." - Jim Rohn

The employers look from among the prospective employees for various types of skills they need depending on their industry and organizational requirements. The list is vast and the same has been trifurcated as follows: self-management skills, job related skills, and transferable skills. The self-management skills are individual specific such as self-discipline, punctuality, work ethics and etiquette to name a few. Employees can carry these skills with themselves for a longer duration. Job related skills differ from industry to industry and organization to organization and these are mostly hard skills. As the name indicates these skills are related to the job they enter. The employees must demonstrate these specific skills to execute the tasks effectively in the workplace. The candidates must display these skills during their interview to grab the employment offer. For instance, the expectations of the IT (Information Technology) industry are different from the banking or pharmaceutical industry. Those who want to join the defence forces must possess various job related qualities such as courage, patriotism, camaraderie, esprit de corps, leadership and communication skills to name a few.

Transferable skills can be transferred from one industry to another industry and from one organization to another organization. Some of the transferable skills are interpersonal skills, communication skills, team spirit, motivation, leadership, problem solving, organizing skills, business communication skills, computer savvy, soft skills, and ability to work without any supervision.

Transferable skills are career transition tools that the employees carry from one industry to another industry. If the employees recognize that they have a flair for another industry in the middle or later part of their career they can shift easily without any difficulty. You can utilize transferable skills in any career. If you present transferable skills properly in your resume it adds value and you will have better chances being shortlisted for an interview.

Soft skills are people skills which are precisely about your personality, attitude and behavior. These skills help communicate with others in a polite and pleasing language. These skills are much sought after currently by all companies globally as it is essential for employees to gel well with their colleagues to work in team dynamics and environment. These skills help the employees survive and succeed in the corporate world. They help employees fast-track their careers and help reach CEO positions quickly. These skills along with conceptual skills are needed at senior management level unlike hard skills which are needed at the low level management. Robert Katz outlined its importance in his classic article, "Skills of an Effective Administrator" (Harvard Business Review, September 1974). He said that when you start your career, to succeed, you need a functional skill: For example, you need to be good at accounting, engineering, or HR. At the next level up, you need to be good with people. And at the very top, you need conceptual skills.

Hence, these soft skills which are part of transferable skills are essential irrespective of the industry, organization and

Time Management

Time management is more about using time judiciously rather than managing time. We all have only 24 hours in a day. We have only one life, and that too is full of complexity and uncertainty. Hence, we must identify our priorities and plan to achieve the desired goals on time. It helps us plan and manage our chores effectively. It helps us minimize pressure and maximize our pleasure. It eliminates stress and ensures work-life balance.

Most of the people are aware that time is more valuable than money as money can be earned, not the lost time. But how to manage time is a million dollar question. You must learn to prioritize tasks so that you focus on important activities rather than insignificant activities. Stephen Covey rightly said, "The key is not to prioritize what's on your schedule, but to schedule your priorities." Most of the time wasters are using internet for long hours and indulging in gossip, spending too much time with visitors and focusing on wrong priorities. Hence, you must address these issues earnestly. When you go by car keep newspapers or books to read as you can invest your commuting time for acquiring knowledge. When someone approaches you and talks about unrelated and superfluous issues you must avoid discussing them. When colleagues come to your cubicle and discuss various issues in the workplace, fix a specific time and indicate the same to them so that they respect your time as well as their time. Here is an elaborative list of 21 timeless tools to manage your time:

21 Timeless Tools to Manage Your Time

"Time is an inelastic resource. No matter how high the demand, we cannot rent, hire or buy more of it."—Peter Drucker

1. Set your goals as goals provide you clarity and put you in a proper direction. In addition, goals remove negative thoughts from your mind and eliminate time robbers. Prepare a "To-Do" list as it helps you organize, prioritize, schedule and act accordingly. But this requires that you first spend your time in meticulous planning. It is worthwhile to invest a part of your time for planning first rather than directly starting to execute the tasks. When you prepare such a list, you are clearly focused and aligned towards your goals. While preparing the list, allow some time for the fact that

things don't always work out as scheduled and there are bound to be some deviations. Of course, the deviations will be minimized when you try to follow the list as closely as possible. Revise your "to-do" list regularly by changing the priorities and eliminating the redundant activities. At the end of the day take a feedback on the execution of all the planned activities. If any major or important activity is left out, you can carry it forward to the next day for execution. And whenever you find any extra time available, you can execute some other action, depending on the priority.

2. Set time for each task. Set a fixed time-frame for completion of each task so that you spend your time wisely. For instance, spend one hour for walking every day, or jogging or at the gym, but don't exceed this time as it will affect other scheduled tasks. Fix some time for checking mails or internet every day, or other important tasks. This will help you focus on your important activities and spend your time judiciously.

3. Find out your biological clock and allocate your time judiciously to reap rewards. Some people can work well in the early morning, some in the noon, and some in the night. If you are a morning person concentrate your morning time on productive and important activities to get the best outcome. You can also execute challenging tasks at this time as both your body and mind supports you to achieve the desired results.

4. Concentrate on core activities. The Pareto principle highlights that people often spend 80 percent of their time that gives 20 percent results, and 20 percent of their time that gives 80 percent results. Hence, address the reasons for spending 80 percent of your time that gives 20 percent results to achieve the desired outcomes, and concentrate on the 20 percent that gives you 80 percent results.

5. Create time logs and find out the time robbers. A time log helps you spot how you spend your entire day and where you waste your precious time. You can check your time robbers to ensure judicious utilization of your time.

6. Be clear in your communication as often people waste their precious time due to miscommunication. Be assertive as well. Learn to say 'No' firmly but politely. Don't oblige unreasonable requests as it takes your personal time and diverts your attention from your roles and responsibilities.

7. Discuss Ideas, not individuals. Plan well ahead with an agenda to conduct your meetings as a lot of time is wasted during meetings. It is rightly said that below average persons discuss individuals, average persons discuss issues and above average persons discuss ideas. When you discuss too much about individuals, you get into unnecessary controversies and into a negative zone. In contrast, when you discuss ideas you get appreciation and command the respect of others as you present yourself as a constructive and creative person. And leaders emphasize more on ideas than on individuals when they troubleshoot or resolve various organizational issues.

8. Recognize that e-mail and paperwork takes a lot of time in the workplace. Hence, keep different e-mail accounts to demarcate your personal, professional and social connections. Check your e-mails from time to time and clear unwanted mails. Use spam filters. Don't subscribe to irrelevant websites. Choose only what is required and subscribe. Similarly, address your paperwork to save your time.

9. Be mentally prepared for crises as crises divert your attention and waste tons of your time. A study reveals[1] that the leaders of any company spend on various issues as per priority as follows: 1 Crises; 2 Telephone calls; 3 Poor planning; 4 Attempting to do too much; 5 Drop-in visitors; 6 Poor delegation; 7 Personal disorganization; 8 Lack of self-discipline; 9 Inability to say 'No'; and finally, 10 Procrastination.

10. Avoid information overload. These days a huge amount of information is available on the internet. Often, people find it tough to differentiate

---

1 http://www.amanet.org/training/books/9780814413388.aspx

between what is necessary and what is unnecessary. John C. Maxwell says in his book *Success - What Every Leader Needs to Know*, "More new information has been produced in the last thirty years than in the previous five thousand. A single weekday edition of the New York Times contains more information than most people in seventeenth-century England were likely to encounter in their lifetimes." A study reveals that now knowledge gets doubled annually, unlike in the 19th century where it took almost 100 years. Too much of information clutters the minds and results in wastage of precious time. It has become a problem of plenty for all of us. For freeing the mind from clutter, Jim Collins says in his book, *Good to Great*[2], "Most of us lead busy, but undisciplined lives. We have ever-expanding 'to do' lists, trying to build momentum by doing, doing, doing—and doing more. And it rarely works. Those who build the good-to-great companies, however, made as much use of 'stop doing' lists as the 'to do' lists. They displayed a remarkable amount of discipline to unplug all sorts of extraneous junk." Hence, avoid

[2] http://books.google.co.in/books?isbn=080101378X

information overload. This will not only save your time but also fine-tune your mind and polish your personality.

11. Manage your mental time. There is a correlation between your thoughts, mental conversations, and actions. Your thoughts will reflect your actions. Don't waste your time thinking about the events of your unpleasant past which cannot be changed now. Studies reveal that people waste 30 per cent of their time thinking about such unpleasant events. Avoid worrying about your future either, as you cannot predict it. Instead, focus on the present on which you have control. In addition, use your inner dialogue effectively. We all have an inner dialogue where we talk to ourselves throughout our waking hours. We must learn to use that time productively by minimizing wastage. This is your mental time management. It is said that success starts from your mind. Similarly, you think within your mind first and then take action. Therefore, make use of your mental time effectively by using efficient time management tools so that you can manage your time better.

This is a wonderful technique to save and manage your time.

12. Use your travel time. You should try to use your travelling time productively. You can read a book or a magazine while travelling or while waiting to meet anyone. You can also check up your emails or read articles on the internet on your areas of interest. You can also use this time to make phone calls to clients or catch up with your old friends or relatives. Enjoy listening to audio recording of your chosen area of interest during your travel time. Some of the senior leaders read newspapers during their travel time. For instance, Jeff Immelt of General Electric and Jeff Bezos of Amazon use their travel time effectively.

13. Think of smart work. Although hard work is essential for achieving the desired outcomes, you must also emphasize on smart work to achieve the outcomes within a limited time-frame. Whenever you want to perform any task, question yourself as to what can be the multiple outcomes out of your efforts and investments. This will help you set the correct priorities and provide solutions to the

tasks. Hence, always question yourself before you start any activity. This will save not only your energy but also your time and money. Shop online preferably to save your time. This is a technology world where there are a number of options to get things done at the click of a mouse. Hence, take the support of technology to save your time, money and energy.

14. Keep reading material with you so that whenever you find time you can read it. Some people spend a lot of time standing in queues; if you are in this situation you can read the material and make use of your time. According to U.S. News & World Report[3] over the course of your lifetime, you will spend eight months opening junk mail, two years unsuccessfully returning phone calls and five years standing in line.

15. Take feedback daily by striking out the activities that have been done and carry forward the left over to the next day. Find out the reasons for not doing the planned tasks. If you find that you have made any mistakes by wasting your time due to

[3] www.rallabandi.in/downloads/Time_Management.pdf

wrong scheduling and prioritizing, ensure that you don't repeat them.

16. Don't procrastinate. Do your tasks regularly as it is rightly said that procrastination is a thief of time. Procrastinators often don't do certain tasks due to various reasons such as fear of failure; fear of criticism; lack of clarity or knowledge; they also avoid tasks that are unpleasant or uninteresting.

17. Avoid distractions. Ensure that you work on your tasks without any distraction. Of course, it is easier said than done in the workplace. But be mentally prepared to execute your tasks to avoid switching costs.

18. Develop people around you so that they can take over a part of your tasks. On one hand, you earn goodwill for developing talent, and on the other, you create time for yourself as you delegate some of your tasks to your people and make them competent and confident.

19. Emphasize similarities, not differences. Employees in the workplace and people in their

personal lives waste their precious time by focusing on differences rather than on similarities which connects them together. When people emphasize on similarities rather than differences, they build bridges, and promote goodwill. In contrast, when people emphasize more on differences of opinions or ideas or views, they build barriers which result in breakup of relationships. In fact, difference in opinions is an indication of independence and freedom among people. Voltaire said, "I may not agree with what you have to say, but I'll defend to my death your right to say it." Hence, we must always respect differences of opinions as people are different and have different emotions, egos, feelings, ideas and insights. Even twins are not alike in their views and ideas. We must always appreciate the different opinions of others. Try to look at similarities rather than differences to maintain healthy relations.

20. Strive for excellence, not perfection. When people emphasize on perfection they waste tons of time. In addition, perfection may not be feasible. Hence, emphasize on excellence.

21. Focus on a single task and avoid multitasking. Although multitasking has both merits and demerits the demerits outnumber the merits as it does not offer satisfactory outcomes. In addition, you incur switching costs. We will discuss next about switching costs in the context.

Account Your Switching Costs

William A. Irwin once said, "Learn to use ten minutes intelligently. It will pay you huge dividends." Hence, those who work in structured jobs must schedule the day well in advance and executive it effectively. However, those who work in unstructured jobs especially middle and senior level managers they find it tough to adopt time-management tools as there are switching costs involved in it.

To manage your time effectively take care of your switching costs. For instance, when you want to do a chore it requires a specific time. Before you start a chore ensure that you have adequate time to do it or else, you waste your time switching from one chore to another. For instance, when you do a task and if there are distractions, you come out of the task to attend to the distraction. Again you need to spend time to reconnect with the task. If you are frequently distracted from doing the task you waste your time connecting back to your task. Leaders at the higher level especially encounter such challenges as they are constantly involved in firefighting and decision-making. Hence, ensure that you have enough time before you start doing a task to avoid being distracted, to save your time and to execute your tasks effectively.

Time is a precious resource everyone is blessed with but you must know how to make use of it. In fact, the richest people on the earth are the poorest in their personal time, and the poorest people on the earth are the richest in their personal time. Both the rich and poor have the richest resource in the earth – time. Thomas Edison rightly quoted, "Time is really the only capital that any human being has, and the only thing he can't afford to lose."

John Maxwell advises to spend 80 percent of the time on work where you are strongest; 15 percent of the time on work where you are learning; and 5 percent of the time on work in other necessary areas. In my case, I spend the morning time to create new content; noon time to generate new content; and night time to destroy irrelevant and outdated ideas in my mind. Hence, I act like a creator in the morning, like Lord Brahma, generator in the noon like Lord Vishnu, and destroyer in the night like Lord Shiva thus playing three roles in a day to utilize my time effectively and provide meaning to my life.

To conclude, time is an irreplaceable resource. Use this precious resource to lead a successful personal, professional and social life. In fact, the biggest gift you can give to others is your time, not money. Remember that if you waste one second, you have wasted one second of your life as God gifted us a limited lifespan.

"Time = Life. Master your time and master your life." - Alan Lakein

Pledge: Manage and master every moment in your life.

References

http://www.amanet.org/training/books/9780814413388.aspx

http://books.google.co.in/books?isbn=080101378X

www.rallabandi.in/downloads/Time_Management.pdf

Smart Leadership: Lessons for Leaders M.S.Rao (2012) Sterling Publishers

Success - What Every Leader Needs to Know, John C. Maxwell

9

Face Corporate Challenges Squarely

"Workplace is a great dynamic. The dynamic between men and women in the workplace is really interesting." - Elizabeth Moss

When students pursue their education in colleges they dream a lot about their jobs and careers with very high expectations. In fact, most of them have higher aspirations and think that it is easy to grab employment opportunities and lead career lives comfortably. Some of the students think that they don't have to learn further after joining employment. But the reality is different. They must learn that the real learning starts in the corporate world. Whatever they learned in education institutions serves as the base and whatever they learn at the workplace sustains their career.

Grabbing employment opportunities is a major challenge and getting adjusted and aligned with the corporate life is even more challenging as there is often a gap between dreams and realities. In fact, corporate life is more challenging as there will be tremendous pressure from all stakeholders including superiors, colleagues, clients, and others. Hence, we will address the challenges the freshers encounter in the initial years of their corporate life. This chapter helps you shift from your campus to corporate life with confidence and to gear up to corporate challenges.

First of all, you may encounter separation from your family and relocation to an unknown place of posting to work. You have to interact with new people in a new location. You must be flexible and adaptable to an alien environment. You must have an open mind to get along with others and adjust with others. It requires a high degree of emotional quotient. This is the major area of challenge.

You must learn the organizational culture and its value system. You must fit into the system to build connectivity and chemistry with the organization. You must develop your emotional intelligence quotient to gel with employees with different cohorts, mindsets, egos, emotions and feelings. It is easier said than done. The best thing for you is to observe how things are run in the company. Listen more and speak less to understand various aspects and to create a positive impact and impression. Precisely, you must develop a positive attitude to learn the corporate ropes.

You must acquire office etiquette and corporate etiquette. Although most of the companies provide induction training programs you must put in extra efforts to acquire etiquette. Usually in the induction training program the companies cover various aspects in breadth such as communication skills, soft skills, corporate culture, organizational culture, HR policies, philosophy of the company, its value system and how it stands out from other organizations. It highlights the organization's vision and mission with historical information of founders and the key people with their names and profiles. It explains the dos and don'ts in the workplace, facilities, pay and perk, dress code, rights and legal issues. In fact, the objective of the induction training program is to help the starters shift to the company quickly and to be productive on the very first day. It serves as a bridge between the new employees and the organization.

Bridge the gap between Gen X (born from 1955 to 1976) and Gen Y (born from 1977 to 1998). You must connect with your seniors who are Gen X with rich experience, knowledge and skills. At times they may have old ideas and insights as they belong to the old school of thought. But be patient to empathize and connect with them. And most of the Gen X also appreciates new ideas and insights from freshers.

You must be prepared to face organizational politics. Although nobody appreciates office politics, often, you are pushed into it either intentionally or unintentionally. Therefore, you must not take any sides in the workplace but mind your own business by contributing your best. Being neutral in the workplace helps you greatly. You must observe who pulls the strings from the front and behind and act accordingly to protect your job and safeguard your career interests. Remember, as long as people are there politics will be there in the workplace. Hence, face office politics with tact and diplomacy.

Sometimes there may not be fixed working hours in the corporate world. The aspirations and expectations of clients and customers are rising rapidly. You must work very hard and smart initially to connect with others to create a good impression, and reap rewards. Remember the slogan: *the more you sweat in peace, less you bleed in war.* Hence, be prepared all the time to project and present yourself as a professional with work ethics and workplace etiquette to stand out from others.

Respect diversity. You come across various employees from different cultures, communities, languages and races in the workplace. You must develop tolerance and respect towards others' communities and cultures. Love your mother but don't hate another person's mother. You must look at similarities by overlooking the differences in others. It creates a broad mindset and you become a true global professional.

To summarize, companies expect several things from freshers especially positive attitude, adaptability, flexibility, absorbability, learnabilty and an urge to embrace change effectively. Hence, you must present the same to build connectivity and chemistry with your company. Remember, if you work hard in the workplace for the first 5 years, you get attuned to it. You will become an expert in your area of interest. You command great respect in the workplace. You don't have to massage your bosses' ego. You can stand out and soar like an eagle.

"Challenges are what make life interesting; overcoming them is what makes life meaningful." - Joshua J. Marine

Pledge: Prepare mentally to face corporate challenges to ensure your survival and success.

10

Build Your Professional Image

"There can be no power without mystery. There must always be a 'something' which others cannot altogether fathom, which puzzles them, stirs them, and rivets their attention.... Nothing more enhances authority than silence. It is the crowning virtue of the strong, the refuge of the weak, the modesty of the proud, the pride of the humble, the prudence of the wise, and the sense of fools."— Charles de Gaulle

When you are ambitious to grow in your career you must impress others with your personality. Personality is a collection of various characteristics and qualities including your physical appearance, charisma, character, communication skills and etiquette. Precisely, personality is all about how you carry yourself. In this chapter we will discuss about building your image effectively to fast-track your career.

Only when you love yourself you will be able to love others. When you want to love yourself you must wear comfortable clothes to appear elegant, groom well and look dignified to stand out from others. When you do so, you add executive presence which is an integral part of charisma.

The image what you think about others perceive you is often different from how others perceive your image. You must learn to bridge the gap between them. You must find out the perceptions of others and create your professional image consistently to impress others. At times your personal appearance and communication skills matter a lot to connect with others. If others are convinced they will take the initiative and you can show your potential, skills and abilities. Hence, it is obvious that external image helps you connect with others quickly while your internal image helps you sustain the relations with others.

As a leader you are always under the scanner at the workplace from various stakeholders such as clients, colleagues, superiors, subordinates, suppliers, financial institutions and government officials depending on the profile and position you hold. Your role is to impress all these stakeholders. People always watch your body language, behavior, communication skills and etiquette.

If you maintain it throughout your professional career you can scale your corporate ladder quickly.

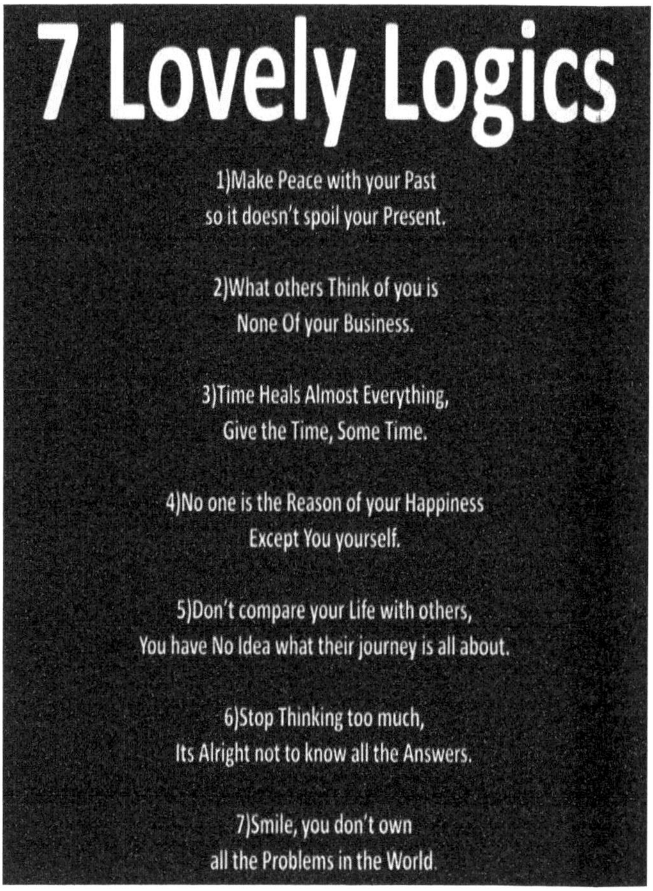

Merits of Building Your Professional Image

You will make more friends. Network and build relations with others quickly. Develop goodwill with all stakeholders quickly. You will be less likely to be pushed into organizational politics. You can add value to your charisma. Above all, you can ensure your professional longevity.

Tools to Build Your Image

Nido Qubein quoted, "Total, unconditional acceptance of yourself is the first step in building a positive self-image." Hence, create your image based on your value system and voice it accordingly through your oral and body language. There should not be any contradiction in it. Your attitude helps immensely to build your professional image. Hence, build your attitude to impress and connect with others. Remember, a professional image built on attitude lasts a longer time than the one built without attitude. Adopt the following tools to build your image:

- If you want to excel with a strong professional image, you must stand by your commitment. You must believe in the slogan - 'promise less and deliver more' to gain credibility from others.
- Win the trust and confidence of others and establish your credibility.
- Improve your communication skills. You must be able to set your personal, professional and social vision and voice it effectively to win others.
- Don't cut corners and compromise with ethics. Even if you fail in other areas people might forgive you but they don't forgive when you emphasize on wrong means to achieve your ends.
- Take the blame in case of failures and spread the fame in case of successes. It helps you gain credibility in the long run although the growth is slow.
- Share your knowledge as knowledge grows when shared. And don't expect anything from others. Remember the slogan 'what goes around comes around'.
- Above all, make a difference in the lives of others.

Hire Image Consultants

Hire image consultants who offer one-on-one and group coaching services. They guide people on optimally using their clothing, grooming and body language including etiquette to inspire confidence in others and create powerful perceptions. There is a huge potential in image consultancy. Most of the professionals and working women are interested in image consultancy. They treat it as an investment, not an expense.

Some celebrities hire image consultants and acquire tools to demonstrate right etiquette and manners in public places. They take tips from image consultants before going to talk shows. Most people observe celebrities in the 'talk shows'. Hence, you must be careful to present a polished and professional image to attract and impress your fans and followers.

Conclusion

People often think that the professional image has to be protected in one organization only. It is a myth. Nowadays, people change organizations and you find your colleagues working there. Whatever impression that you have created in the previous organization will be carried forward to your next organization. Hence, guard your professional image. Take the initiative to build your personal and professional image at the workplace. If you neglect this aspect your professional career will be at stake. Be sensible about what you talk with others and how you walk your talk. Out of 10 qualities, people often have the habit of forgetting your 9 good qualities but are eager to highlight your one weakness. Hence, be conscious about your image and take all precautions to present and project a positive image to ensure lasting career success.

"The full measure of a man is not to be found in the man himself, but in the colors and textures that come alive in others because of him." - Albert Schweitzer

Pledge: Build and protect your professional image.

11

Influence Others with the "Mirroring Technique"

"You can make more friends in two months by becoming interested in other people than you can in two years by trying to get other people interested in you." - Dale Carnegie

Everyone wants to influence others and make more friends as it is one of the basic human needs. However, everyone will not succeed; only a few succeed to impact others. You can use the 'mirroring technique' to connect and influence others. The mirroring technique is all about changing your language and behavior during conversations as per the other persons to connect with them quickly as per the situation.

When you are in a public gathering or group, observe the ambience and get into the situation with a flexible mindset and an open mind. Listen to the people closely, observe the way they talk, and focus on the topic. Display your authentic interest to listen to others. Nod your head in agreement with a cheerful note to get an entry into it. Depending on the situation, or when one of the persons makes a long pause during the conversation, take the initiative and express your viewpoints precisely. If you disagree with the views of the other person, express them with etiquette in a polite and pleasing manner. If you agree with their viewpoint, you can express the same by including a few more points.

Methodology of the Mirroring Technique

Here is how the mirroring technique works: You must mirror as per the other person based on body language, voice modulation, and oral language and as per the prevailing ambience. You must mould your body language, voice modulation and oral language as per the other person and reciprocate accordingly to create compatibility and chemistry. It requires a lot of practice to adopt the mirroring technique. But it is easy to adopt when you are aware of this technique. All that you need is to possess a positive attitude and an open mindset to connect with others. If you become an expert in this technique you can influence and inspire others.

The mirroring technique helps in many ways. For instance, leaders like Lincoln and Churchill practiced their presentation in front of the mirror to gain confidence and delivered amazing speeches which are memorable even today. This is an amazing tool to enhance your confidence levels to work well and address the audience effectively to achieve the desired outcomes. Learn, practice, and apply this technique to achieve great success in your life.

'Winner and Mirror' Technique

"Aim at heaven and you will get earth thrown in. Aim at earth and you get neither." - Clive Staples Lewis

The mirroring technique helps reprogram your subconscious mind as well. You can build confidence and continuously motivate yourself with this great tool. When you find the lows in life; go inside the room; close the door; stand in front of the mirror; smile and shout aloud, 'I am the winner' repeatedly for a few minutes. It changes the way you think as it lifts your energy and confidence levels instantly. The technique here is that when you hear your own voice with positive messages your mind gets reinforced with positive vibes. Secondly, you also see your face smiling in the mirror thus enhancing your self-esteem. Hence, there is a twin effect on your mind and face culminating in getting out of depression and getting into an energetic and confidence mode. I advised this technique to many of my participants in my leadership training programs and it worked wonders. I received great response as people bounced back from failures and depression and achieved great success in their lives.

To summarize, there are innumerable advantages out of the mirroring technique. You can reprogram your subconscious mind; enhance your self-esteem; and self-confidence. You can impact and influence others to make friends. You can inspire others to become a great orator. Hence, understand and apply this tool to achieve all-round success in your life.

"Perhaps you will forget tomorrow the kind words you say today, but the recipient may cherish them over a lifetime."
- Dale Carnegie

Pledge: Adopt the 'Mirroring Technique' to win friends and influence others.

12

Fast-track Your Career with Hard and Soft Skills

"If words of command are not clear and distinct, if orders are not thoroughly understood, the general is to blame. But if his orders are clear, and the soldiers nevertheless disobey, then it is the fault of their officers." - Sun Tzu

When you look at leaders like Ronald Reagan, former President of America, Carly Fiorina, former boss of Hewlett Packard, Steve Jobs of Apple, and Vikram Pandit ex-CEO of Citibank group they all had one common thread connecting them. They all were asked to leave from their jobs. Vikram Pandit was asked to leave as he had a problem with board members and stakeholders. He missed something to make a mark in his career. He was placed at the top slot due to his hard skills but asked to leave due to dearth of soft skills despite delivering better corporate results. People often don't take soft skills seriously as they treat it like any other skill. When you look at Steve Jobs he was fired from Apple due to dearth of soft skills but was invited to join again due to his hard skills when the company was in trouble. Commenting on his ouster from Apple Steve said, "It was awful-tasting medicine, but I guess the patient needed it. Sometimes life's gonna hit you in the head with a brick. Don't lose faith." Steve Jobs learned lessons from the ouster and developed some degree of soft skills and since then there was no looking back, and he branded himself as an innovation legend. In this context, we will discuss about hard and soft skills.

Hard versus Soft Skills

Hard skills are the academic skills and technical skills. It is about technical acumen including knowledge, skills and abilities. It is also about technical competence and capability and what value you have. In contrast, soft skills are non-academic skills such as interpersonal skills, people skills and life skills that help you share your academic and technical skills effectively. Hence, soft skills are the polite and pleasing way of communicating with others to influence others to get the tasks executed effectively. It demonstrates your personality, attitude and behavior to others to influence impact and impress others. These are beyond interpersonal, team-building, and communication skills although they are a subset of soft skills. Precisely, soft skills help you present your hard skills successfully. Hence, there is a great connection between these two skills. People ignore soft skills at their peril.

We can also define soft skills as the polite and pleasing way of communicating and getting across the message to others successfully. Here is an example that differentiates between hard and soft skills.

"Don't use my telephone."
"Thanks for not using my telephone."

Although the two sentences convey the same message the second sentence sounds more convincing and pleasing than the first one. The first sentence conveyed "what" the message was while the second sentence conveyed "how" the message was. Hence, the first sentence can be compared with hard skills while the second sentence with soft skills as it was polite and pleasing for others to listen and change their behavior.

Soft skills focus on how we communicate while hard skills emphasize on what we communicate. Although it sounds and appears to be the same there is a thin line that separates them - that is a pleasant and pleasing tone of communication. Hence, communication skill is an ingredient of soft skills but not per se soft skills. Hence, soft skills are all about how you carry yourself with your personality and how you respond to the situation through positive, right and strong attitude, and how you behave in the situation. If you behave positive you get positive results. If people behave negative they get negative results. Here is how you can differentiate between hard and soft skills:

- Hard skills are mostly tangible while the soft skills are mostly intangible.
- Hard skills depend on the type of the trade and industry one is into while soft skills depend on the type of people they handle and the organizational culture they are into. Hard skills remain more or less the same while the soft skills change as per the people, situation and organizational set-up.
- Hard skills can be taught by the teachers in the educational institutions while soft skills can be trained by trainers in the corporate world. However, the awareness about soft skills can be made in the educational institution.
- Hard skills are about the knowledge of the subject while soft skills are about the personality, attitude

and behavioral aspects. Hence, hard skills can be more easily measured than soft skills. In addition, hard skills are easy to identify and can be measured with accuracy while soft skills are tough to identify and cannot be measured with accuracy.

- Most of the careers need both hard and soft skills. There are very few careers where soft skills are least required and where group activities are not involved. For careers that need more of group activities and dynamics, there is need for more soft skills.

Advantages of Soft Skills

Soft skills are the thin line that separates success and failure, and professional survival and success. Here are some of the merits of being equipped with soft skills:

- Connects with the corporates quickly as the corporates want plug and play candidates.
- Enhances employability among candidates as it conveys the right attitude and personality and displays good behavior during the interview.
- Builds good relations with others.

- Eliminates conflicts at the workplace and minimizes attrition.
- Promotes networking skills.
- Ensures quick career success.

A Case Study on Soft and Hard Skills

"A thing of beauty is a joy forever: Its loveliness increases; It will never pass into nothingness." — John Keats

I attended the annual day celebrations of a college and was returning home in their college bus. I was very excited about the way the annual day was celebrated, and I especially enjoyed speeches delivered by prestigious personalities. A woman faculty member from a women's college sitting behind me in the college bus started to criticize the management of the educational institution for not giving any prizes to their girl students. Her girl students were sitting around her. She also criticized in the presence of her girl students that the girls from her college were used by the management of the educational institution to give away awards to noted personalities on the dais. I felt very bad about the kind of language she used in the bus about girl students and that too in front of them.

I realized that the woman faculty member was upset with the management and unhappy that none of her girl students received any prizes. I intervened with a smile and said to her:

Instead of thinking that the girls from your college were used by the management, think with a positive perception that the girls from your college are so beautiful that they were invited to give away bouquets and awards to the dignitaries on the dais. After listening to my comment the girl students felt happy. Secondly, I told the woman faculty member to think and say as follows: "The girls from our women's college are so broadminded that they give away awards to others and don't expect any prizes from others. Without the active participation of beautiful girls from our college the annual day celebrations will be incomplete."

The woman faculty member smiled and felt happy with the way I presented to her statements in a positive light and the girls were so excited with my compliment. And all of us travelled back home by the college bus with sweet memories.

From this case study it is obvious that the woman faculty member presented through hard skills but I presented the same through soft skills. Additionally, everything depends on the way we look at things. If you look positively everything looks positive; and if you look negatively, everything looks negative. George Harrison rightly quoted, "It's all in the mind." Remember the slogan: "We see the world the way we are, not the way they are." Convert your mindset from complaining to compliment to make the people around you happy. Above all, communicate through soft skills rather than through hard skills.

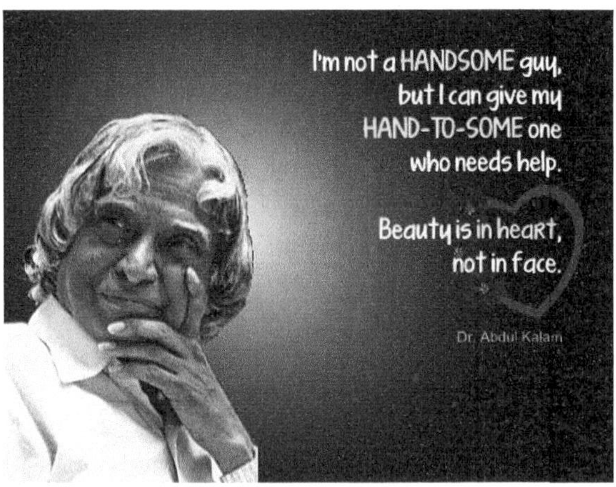

Hard and Soft Skills Make You a Smart Leader

If you have hard skills, you will be hired and if you don't have soft skills you will be fired. That means you must possess hard skills to get hired, and you must acquire soft skills to avoid getting fired. Hence, blend hard and soft skills proportionately to achieve professional success. In addition, you can grow in your professional life as a leader exponentially when you can effectively blend these skills. When you can blend hard and soft skills successfully you can excel as a smart leader who is able to articulate knowledge across to others and also to get the tasks executed effectively.

Soft skills are associated with Emotional Quotient (EQ) and hard skills are associated with Intelligence Quotient (IQ). It is a bit hard to acquire Intelligence Quotient (IQ) but it is easy to acquire Emotional Quotient (EQ). The good news is that you already have IQ. Now it is time for you to acquire EQ and blend it effectively to scale your corporate ladder quickly.

Hard and Soft Skills and Left and Right-Brain

According to Nobel Laureate, Roger W. Sperry, the human brain is divided into two compartments (hemispheres) - "left-brained" and "right-brained". Those who are "left-brained" are often said to be more logical, analytical and objective while those who are "right-brained" are said to be more intuitive, thoughtful and subjective. The left-brainers are good at words and language and can understand effectively. They can design strategies and be practical in approach and execution. In contrast, the right-brainers are highly imaginative and can see the big picture. They appreciate spatial perception and are good at conceptual skills. The left-brain tends to break down information for analysis, while the right-brain tends to put information together to create a whole picture. Precisely, left-brainers are smart in technical acumen while the right-brainers are good at social acumen as it deals with interpersonal skills. Since the left-brain involves with logic and language where people prefer to work with less interaction, hard skills fall in this bracket. Since the right-brain is creative and imaginative and involves group dynamics and activities, soft skills fall in this bracket. Hence, left-brainers are often smart in technical acumen and hard skills while the right-brainers are often good at social acumen and soft skills.

Book Smart versus Street Smart

People who are book smart are often good at hard skills but they find it tough to be good at soft skills as soft skills involve group dynamics. What is written in the books is quite different from the real corporate world. Hence, book smarts fail to become street smarts and often don't possess the requisite soft skills thus hitting lows in their careers. Similarly, when we look at some of the leadership researchers and educators who are great at their hard skills and groom leaders fail miserably in their real lives to excel as leaders due to dearth of soft skills. In contrast, most of the corporate leaders possess soft skills due to frequent group interaction and experience but don't possess requisite knowledge of hard skills. Hence, there must be a judicious mix of hard and soft skills to survive in one's personal, professional and social life.

Blend Hard and Soft Skills at all Levels

"The softest things in the world overcome the hardest things in the world." - Lao-tzu

Blending both hard and soft skills helps fast-track your career. Here is the formula blending them:

Hard Skills + Soft Skills = Quick Career Growth

Soft skills help leaders get the tasks executed successfully. Hence, leaders must acquire soft skills to articulate effectively with others and execute the tasks successfully. As they reach higher positions they need more of soft skills. According to Robert Katz, there are three levels of management such as low, middle and top level. When you join at the entry level you must possess a high of hard and low of soft skills. When you come to the middle level you must possess an equal amount of hard and soft skills. When you go to the top level management, you must possess a low of hard skills and a high of soft skills. Hence, it is obvious that these skills are essential irrespective of the levels of management but the need for soft skills increases as you reach senior positions.

Change in Mindset

Globally the trend changed from being competitive to collaborative. Hence, there must be a change in the mindset of the people and to achieve the same, soft skills play a crucial role. Currently corporate culture shifted from vertical to horizontal and Gen Y appreciates collegial mode of relationship where there is not much gap between the superiors and subordinates. To go further, Gen Y appreciates partnerships rather than the traditional command-and-control managerial hierarchy and relationship. The knowledge workers who are very smart with unique ideas and insights prefer to work with freedom and independence. And to get the job done by them effectively, soft skills play a crucial role. Hence, currently there is a growing significance of soft skills and leaders are taking more interest to develop these skills among themselves and also for others to enhance leadership effectiveness and success.

Conclusion

People enter the corporate world due to hard skills and succeed due to soft skills. If they don't equip themselves with soft skills they fall flat from the corporate ladder. Hence, it is essential to emphasize on soft and hard skills to ensure and achieve professional success. However, when you want to scale up the corporate ladder quickly, you must acquire more of soft skills as your hard skills may not matter much over a period of your professional career. Hence, blend hard and soft skills to fast-track your career and emphasize more on soft skills to scale senior positions quickly.

Pledge: Blend hard and soft skills to excel as a smart leader.

13

Be a Change Leader

"A change leader looks for change, knows how to find the right changes and knows how to make them effective both outside the organization and inside it." - Peter F Drucker.

When we look at leaders like Jack Welch, Carlos Ghosn, Lou Gerstner and C. Martinez we find one thing common among them. They are all change leaders who effected change successfully and turned around their organizations. They encountered several challenges during organizational changes and finally, came out with flying colors. They brought laurels to their organizations and are acclaimed as great organizational leaders. Their journey of leadership was beset with both bouquets and brickbats. Neither bouquets elevated them nor did brickbats prevent them from leading change.

What is Change?

Change is all about status quo ante. The 21st century has brought several challenges and changes in the business world such as uncertainty and complexity arising out of rapid changes in technologies. It has become impossible to predict where technology would take us to the next level thus making the change process highly complicated. Organizations are forced to bring out change due to fierce competition. They strive to bring out new products and procedures to make their businesses relevant and vibrant. They look for innovative means and methodologies to stay ahead of others.

Types of Change

There are several types of change. According to Linda Ackerman there are three types of change. The first type of change is developmental change. This refers to improving what already exists in the organization. This is the same as convergence, incremental or evolutionary change on models of organizational change. The second type of change is transitional change which involves moving from the current state to a known new state through a transition state. Re-structuring, mergers, introduction of new processes, technologies, systems and procedures are examples of transitional change. In transitional change, the organization retains some of its old aspects and adds on new ones. The third type of change is called transformational change. This type of change is a fundamental re-invention of the organization including changes in its leadership, mission, culture, structure, strategy, and human resource practices.

What is Change Management?

As individuals undergo change, the organizations also undergo change. For human beings, there are three stages - birth, growth and death. However, for organizations there are five stages - birth, growth, transformation, decline and death. Organizations must not vanish over a period of time. Hence, when the decline is anticipated, it is essential for managers and leaders to turnaround their organizations through various strategies to ensure that the organizational graph goes in the northward direction.

Change management can be defined as the process of effecting changes in a systematic, structured and sequential manner for transforming the organizations from uncertainty to certainty when encountered with volatility, uncertainty, complexity and ambiguity due to rapid changes in technology. It calls for effective leadership, value-based leadership and principle-centered leadership to achieve organizational transformation effectively. In a nutshell, change management is all about effecting changes in the organization to enhance organizational excellence and effectiveness. It is the process of managing change effectively and efficiently through innovative tools and techniques without inviting any resistance.

Is Change Essential?

It is imperative to embrace change as the world is changing rapidly due to technology. For instance, IBM and GE not only survived but also excelled as top class companies as the change leaders realized and turned around their organizations when the companies were on the verge of extinction.

On the human front, people change with changing times and technologies covering their personal, professional and social life. Nobody is immune to change. It is next to impossible to avoid change. For instance, man is born as a child, and grows as an adolescent, teenager, adult, middle aged, old aged and finally, departs this world. In a nutshell, man changes from womb to tomb. Similarly, the organizations must change with the changing times and technologies.

Currently the demands of the customers are changing rapidly. It has become a tough task to meet their aspirations and expectations. Companies constantly innovate to catch up with changing customer tastes and preferences. They resort to creativity and innovation to stand out from the pack and beat the competition. Hence, change is essential for growth.

Is Change Different From Growth?

There is often confusion between change and growth. However, there is a vast difference between them. People talk of seeking change mistaking change for growth. A few individuals say that they want change in their careers. In fact, they should be clear whether they are vexed with their existing careers and want to shift to another career or grow in their careers by shifting from one place to another.

People, at times, get impatient about growth. The fact is that growth cannot happen overnight. It takes time and requires tons of efforts and energies. In contrast, change may take place overnight. Growth is a gradual process. Change could be for better or worse. However, growth is for the better. Growth could be in a particular area. Change could be at an overall perspective.

Growth means stepping into known areas whereas change means stepping from known to unknown areas. Change happens automatically. In contrast, growth takes place intentionally through hard work, smart work and network.

However, one thing is common between change and growth, both involve coming out of the comfort zone into an effective zone.

Why Do People Resist Change?

Everyone is scared of change. When we talk of changing clothes, food habits and lifestyles, we get excited. However, when we are asked to change location, and the nature of work or roles and responsibilities and policies and procedures, we often get stressed. Why is it so? Does it not sound contradictory? But it is a fact that people resist change. In this context, let us find out the reasons for resistance and the role of leaders in minimizing resistance.

- When people don't have competency and qualifications, they fear change. Hence, the onus lies with leaders to build competency levels among their people for effecting change smoothly.
- When people are scared of the workload, they resist change. Hence, leaders must allay their apprehensions by adjusting their workload.
- Often people may doubt the inner motives of their leaders and resist. Therefore, the leaders

must build trust and confidence among their people.

- People may have apprehensions about losing monetary benefits or social status or designations. The leaders must provide assurances for the same. They must communicate with people clearly that not changing in line with the external environment is riskier than embracing change.

Change Leadership

The problem with people is that they assume that status quo is good. Many are cynical about change as change involves lots of uncertainty and complexity. Even though the current scenario may not be ideal, people still prefer to remain without change as they think that a known devil is better than an unknown angel. Here comes the role of change leaders who need to build confidence among the people about the merits of wedding change and shedding what is not good for the organization.

Change leadership is the process of effecting change successfully by neutralizing the anti-change forces and persuading the people to fall in line for their prosperity and that of the organization. It calls for allaying the apprehensions of the people who have reservations and eliminating the people who are against change due to vested interests.

While managing change we find three categories of people: actors, spectators and speed brakers. Actors are the people who have positive attitude with loads of initiative and energy to proceed as per the plans of the change leaders. Spectators are the people who are undecided about the change with reservations, apprehensions, and queries. Finally, speed brakers are the people who constantly protest and are dead against change. Generally we find a small percentage of people falling in the bracket of actors and speed brakers while the majority fall in the category of spectators. At times, speed brakers endeavor to divert the attention of the spectators and indulge in cultivating an anti-change mindset. Hence, the change leadership calls for persuading the spectators and ensuring that the speed brakers don't scuttle the change process. The change leaders must demonstrate great patience, tact and toughness to handle the speed brakers.

Leadership is one of the influential levers that help bring out change successfully. It plays a crucial role is managing change effectively. If the leaders are visionary and trustworthy the people express their confidence to follow and support the change process wholeheartedly.

While managing change, the leaders must clear confusion through open communication. They must appreciate the feelings and fears of employees and move accordingly. They must set hope as it guides people with confidence. They must clearly state the vision.

To make the change process successful, change leaders must know the motivational needs of their people.

Change leaders must walk the talk during the change process. They should be with the people throughout the change process to clear their queries and apprehensions to build trust and confidence.

Change leaders must provide passion and a strong sense of purpose about change. They must share their power. They must share the vision with their employees so that they feel that they are an integral part of the change process. They must sell out during the entire change process.

According to Kotter, "Do not declare victory too soon". Ensure that change take place completely as anything can happen during the course of change, consolidation and implementation. For instance, new bottlenecks may crop up and fresh resistance may surface that upsets the change applecart. The anti-changers are always active; they are out to upset the change process. It is essential not to underestimate their might.

Change is full of surprises. Quick change is always counterproductive. During the process of change, the change leaders must weigh the pros and cons and take a calculated and practical approach for successful implementation.

While effecting change, the leaders must focus on the internal and external environment simultaneously as both are interrelated. When the internal environment demands change, the leaders must prepare and effect change. This is an easier process as things are within the control of leaders. However, when there is need from the external environment to manage change, it becomes a Herculean task for leaders to manage change.

The external environment factors include political, economic, governmental social and technological factors. Internal environment factors include strategic requirements to beat competition and routine planning based on resources and or other factors.

According to Lippit (Lippit, 1959) the four 'golden rules' that the change agent has to observe are:

Rule 1: The nature of the relationship.

Rule 2: To initiate an organization development process within any organization, the change agent has to help solve a current or potential problem.

Rule 3: The relationship is a temporary one and the change agent and the organization must accept the temporary nature of the assistance being provided.

Rule 4: The change agent must be an outsider who is not part of the hierarchical power system in which the client organization is located.

Characteristics of Change Leaders

The study of 90 leaders in USA by Warren Bennis and Burt Nanus reveal that all leaders shared five key skills: They are

1. The ability to accept people as they are, not as you would like them to be, so that you truly understand what other people are like on their terms.
2. The capacity to approach people and problems in terms of the present rather than the past, and thus

free yourself from the preoccupation with rehashing things that are over.

3. The ability to treat those who are close to you with the same courteous attention that you extend to strangers and casual acquaintances, and thus avoid misunderstandings, misconceptions and mistakes.
4. The ability to trust others, even if the risk seems great, without assuming that most people are incompetent and insincere.
5. The ability to do without constant approval and recognition from others, and thus being free to take appropriate risks without undue preoccupation with being a 'good guy'.

Today's business world is highly fierce and there is no room for mistakes. Any small mistake might prove to be costly for the organizations. Hence, the change leaders must demonstrate certain characteristics that are unique and far different from the conventional leadership.

Change requires flexible leaders who can adapt to various situations and styles and people to manage the change successfully. As leadership begins and ends with example, the change leaders must set an example for the people right from the beginning to the end of the change process.

They must have strong visionary skills and must be clear where they are taking their people. It makes things clear for people and implementation of change becomes easier. They must walk and talk and must complement both in words and deeds with change to create trust among the people.

They must possess strong communication skills to get across the message clearly to clear any apprehensions about change. It is essential to remove obstacles in the change process. They must demonstrate firefighting and troubleshooting skills during the process of change.

They must empower others, share vision, motivate others, and make change an integral part of organizational culture. They must always have the attitude of *'we can do it'* and must be highly focused and always do the right things rather than things right.

They must have charisma to empathize with their people and listen attentively to develop others. They must communicate in simple and plain language and present change through visual pictures to get across the message effectively.

They must be confident and competent. They must have sound judgment based on the past successes, failures and intuition. They must learn to prioritize the tasks and strictly focus on the change efforts. It is also essential to show and celebrate small successes to motivate others.

They must be risk takers and learn to overcome bureaucratic bottlenecks during the process of change. They must create common ground wherein the people focus on commonalities rather than differences. They must have a burning desire to effect change. In other words, they must be highly passionate and to achieve the same, they must associate and align people who are highly passionate in effecting change.

They must be strong in emotional intelligence. Daniel Goleman wrote about emotional intelligence wherein emotional intelligence is the major factor that differentiates leaders from followers.

They must be good at analytical and problem solving skills by looking at the big picture. Above all, the change leaders must be passionate in their endeavors to effect change smoothly and successfully.

Peters and Waterman (1982) and Kanter (1983; 1989) suggest that there are common culturally related attributes associated with organizations recognized as being masters of change. The attributes may be presented as follows:

1. A clear and communicated strategic vision
2. Visible senior management involvement
3. People-based competitive edge
4. Marketing ethos
5. Consensus-driven management
6. Awareness and reflection of social responsibility

Conclusion

Jack Welch once said, "If the rate of change on the outside exceeds the rate of change on the inside, the end is near." The only thing constant in the corporate world is change and competition. Every change is made for a reason. Every change is decided upon because the positives of the change outweigh the negatives. Nobody can survive without change. Hence, everyone must change with the changing times and technologies to grow personally, professionally and socially.

Change is inevitable. Change is the mantra for survival and success. The business scenario is changing rapidly and the organizations need to keep pace with the same and reinvent and evolve accordingly to achieve organizational excellence and effectiveness.

The river that goes to the sea undergoes several changes during the course of the journey; it is sometimes slow and sometimes swift as per the situation in its journey. So is the case with human life. Throughout human life, man undergoes several challenges such as peaks, valleys, smooth and rough terrains. The only successful people are the ones who accept and mould themselves as per the changing environment.

Change can be stressful, painful and helpful. It all depends on how you view change. If you accept change with optimism it can be helpful. In contrast, if you view change with cynicism it will be painful as well as stressful. Hence, welcome change wholeheartedly to ensure survival and achieve success in all walks of your life.

If there were no changes, mankind would have remained in the Stone Age. Hence, let us mentally prepare to shed the old outdated practices and procedures and wed new ones that lead to all-round peace and prosperity.

"Change is inevitable in a progressive society. Change is constant." - Benjamin Disraeli

Pledge: Embrace change to excel as an effective leader.

References

Change Management – A guide to effective implementation authored by Robert A. Paton and James McCalman (Publishers - Response Books- Sage Publications)

Managing Organizational Change authored by V.Nilakant and S.Ramnarayan (Publishers - Response Books- Sage Publications)

Management Challenges for the 21st century by Peter Ferdinand Drucker

14

Raise Your Bar Constantly

"To be a successful boxer one must also have a strong heart. Some women are physically strong but fail when it comes to having a strong heart. One also must have the zeal and the right fighting spirit." - Mary Kom.

Everyone wants to grow and achieve success in their lives. They must raise their bars constantly to make it big in life. By the way 'what do you mean by raising the bar?' 'Raising the bar' means to do better than the past. It is about competing with oneself to deliver better results. It is setting higher standards to provide meaning to one's life. Succinctly, it is about excellence. We can take the example of Mary Kom in this regard.

Mary Kom – Raising her Bar Constantly

"We work harder than men and are determined to fight with all our strength to make our nation proud. God has given me the talent and it's only because of sheer grit and hard work that I have made it so far." - Mary Kom

Mangte Chungneijang Mary Kom from Manipur is an ideal example of constantly raising her bar to make it big in Boxing. Mary Kom is married to K Onler Kom and is a mother of twin sons - Rechungvar and Khupneivar. She made India proud by winning the bronze medal in Boxing in the London Olympics 2012. She has received many awards including the Arjuna Award, the Padma Shri Award, the Rajiv Gandhi Khel Ratna Award and a special award from AIBA.

Mary surprised everyone by making it big through her discipline and dedication. Nothing stopped her reaching to the top slot - Neither her gender, height, region, poverty nor motherhood. She rightly said, "Don't give up as there is always a next time. Think that if Mary Kom, a mother of two, can do it, why can't you?" Mary Kom overcame several challenges including gender bias, poverty, being small in size, that is 5' 2" in height, and that too hailing from a small region like Manipur by raising her bar constantly; you too can make it big in your life if you break your mental barriers.

Many felt that Mary was finished after troubled times at the national level. But she practiced and bounced back.

She constantly raised her bar and achieved success through years of hard work, dedication, determination and single-minded focus. She is not resting on her laurels and getting complacent. She is constantly raising her bar to win gold in the 2016 Rio Olympics.

Mary Kom

Tips to Raise Your Bar

Raising the bar is not about competing with others. When you compete with others you may develop negative energies whereas when you compete with yourself you develop positive energies thus building your self-esteem and unlocking your hidden potential. Hence, you need to raise your bar constantly by competing with yourself. Here are the tips to raise your bar:

- Get into your passionate areas. Work hard, smart and wise.
- Read continuously and acquire knowledge, skills and abilities.
- Join professional organizations where you can meet people of your professional expertise to grow. It helps you understand the developments taking place in your domain and also to raise your bar constantly.
- Stay away from your comfort zone and get into an effective zone.
- Learn, unlearn and relearn. This is the world of uncertainty and complexity. The globe is undergoing transformation rapidly, and to catch up with it, update yourself and reinvent yourself.

Remember 3Cs – Comparing, Competing and Collaborating

It is rightly said, "Why compare yourself with others? No one in the entire world can do a better job of being you than you." Hence, don't compare and compete with others. But collaborate with others. Remember these 3Cs – comparing, competing and collaborating. When you compare with others it brings down your self-esteem; when you compete with others it generates envy and ill-will. In contrast, when you collaborate you respect others' strengths and capitalize them for mutual growth and prosperity. It provides you with a win-win situation thus projecting you as a leader. You can also compete with yourself, but not with others. When you compete with yourself you develop a competitive spirit and come out of your comfort zone and continuously stay in your effective zone. Those who are super achievers and high performers, constantly remain in their effective zones. When they find that their effective zones turn out to be comfort zones they shift their orbit quickly into new zones. Hence, comparing with others is counterproductive, competing with yourself is productive, and collaborating with others is highly productive. When you want to grow quickly in this rapidly changing technological world you must learn to be flexible and accommodate others and reinvent yourself regularly to leave a mark behind for others to follow.

God created everyone with unique talents and gifts. You must know what you have been blessed with so that you can grow with such talents by setting your goals. Hence, take inventory of your strengths and weaknesses and leverage your strengths by overcoming your weaknesses. Remember to be original and creative rather than being a copycat and follower.

I always compete with myself in my life. I don't take anybody as my role model. I work hard, smart and wise all the time to grow in my life and to serve my students. I learn continuously and take feedback from others constantly to raise my own bar and grow professionally.

Remember that even twins are not alike in behavior and performance although they have the same genes because the personality of an individual depends not only on heredity, but also environment and situation. Hence, it is counterproductive to compare and compete with others. The only wise option for you is to collaborate and grow collectively to provide meaning to your life, and to make a difference in the lives of others.

"Nobody can make you feel inferior without your consent." - Eleanor Roosevelt

Pledge: Compete with yourself to raise your bar constantly.

15

Do Your Duty; Rewards will Follow

"Do what best you can do today thinking that there is no tomorrow. While learning think that you live longer and while sharing knowledge think that today is the last day in life. You will never be happy if you continue to search for what happiness consists of. You will never live if you are looking for the meaning of life." - Albert Camus

There are people who look at rewards rather than putting their efforts. There are people who put efforts and look

for instant outcomes. There are people who put in their efforts and wait for results to come. There are people who invest their efforts and don't bother for rewards. Which category do you belong?

If you belong to the fourth category you are the right person to lead happily in this world without any concerns. Unfortunately, most people belong to the first, second and third categories. Lord Shri Krishna preached in the epic Mahabharata, "Do your duty; reward is not thy concern." That means, man must put in his efforts and should not concern himself about the outcomes. God gave us life and our duty is to work the best way we can because He is there to take care of us.

When Abraham Lincoln was delivering his speech he was spotted by a member of the Republican Party in America and was asked to contest the Presidential elections. Republicans never tasted political power in America until then. They were on the look out for the right candidate to lead the party as the country was in major challenges at that time. They liked Lincoln's humble background and his oratory skills, and chose him to lead the party. Lincoln contested elections and won. He became the first Republican to become the President of America.

For Abraham Lincoln, delivering speeches was part of his duty, and he did it with excellence. For Lincoln, excellence was an attitude and whatever he undertook he did his best. The essence of this example is to do your job properly so that you will be spotted and slotted at the right place and at the right time thus achieving success and touching your tipping point in life. Similarly, Barack Obama was spotted by Democrats and was asked to lead the party as he rose from humble origins. He was also a great orator, and believed in delivering his best unmindful of the outcomes. His excellence in his work led him to lead second term as the President of America.

From the examples of these two American Presidents it becomes clear that everyone has to do their work sincerely. And results will follow naturally thus overcoming tons of trials and tribulations people undergo in their lives. In my professional life, I follow Winston Churchill's message - "We make a living by what we get, but we make a life by what we give." I deliver my best as a teacher, trainer and author to make a difference in the lives of others. It gives me great satisfaction and provides meaning to my life.

To conclude, do your best irrespective of the industry or the sector or the area you are into without overly concentrating on your outcomes. And I am sure you will find amazing outcomes one fine day which would outshine the tons of trials and tribulations that you had undergone during your lifetime, finally taking you to the top of the world.

"You must have control of the authorship of your own destiny. The pen that writes your life story must be held in your own hand." - Irene C. Kassorla

Pledge: Emphasize on your efforts and outcomes will follow accordingly.

16

Industry Prefers Deployable Students to Employable Students

"In today's knowledge-based economy, what you earn depends on what you learn. Jobs in the information technology sector, for example, pay 85 percent more than the private sector average." - Bill Clinton

Most of the students who pass out from educational institutions are not employable currently. They prepare from the exams' perspective and come out with grades through rote learning and cramming the content without understanding the subject. It results in unemployability among the students. They complain that the government is not providing them with jobs. They must understand that industry looks for plug and play candidates who can be productive on the very first day. They must appreciate that there are certain skills required that help them grab employment opportunities such as soft skills and employability skills. In fact, companies are looking for deployable students rather than employable students. Deployable students are the students who can work in the corporate world without much training except through induction programs. Companies don't appreciate spending money in training the employable students as costs involved are high. Hence, educational institutions must prepare deployable students to enhance campus placements.

Educators must encourage their students to improve their communication skills as most of the students hail from a rural background. Educators must ask students what they have learnt at the end of each session as it helps students improve their communication skills and also helps educators assess whether students understood the content in the classroom. It is the role of educators to enlighten students about the industry expectations and the current challenges students are facing so that students can work hard seriously to become employable and deployable at the corporate world.

Parents must also encourage their children to acquire other skills apart from academic skills to enhance employability and fast-track their careers. They must take time off from their busy schedules and ask their children to deliver a presentation once in a week of what they learned in the classroom. It helps them improve their communication skills, acquire command over the subject and build their confidence.

Currently companies spend a significant amount in the name of corporate social responsibility. They must undertake the initiative to address the challenge of unemployablity among the Indian students. They must pick up passionate industry experts who want to make a difference in the lives of students and send them to educational institutions to bring awareness about the industry expectations and the customers' aspirations. These industry experts must inform academia about the rapidly changing expectations of the custormers and implore the latter to design the course curriculum accordingly and deliver to students. These industry experts must also conduct guest lectures; gauge the pulse of the students; and report back to industry with their feedback. It enables the industry to prepare its induction programs and corporate training programs as per the intelligence level of the students to bridge the gap between the campus and industry. Hence, there must be a right chemistry between the campus and the corporate.

Non-Governmental Organizations (NGOs) must take the initiative with the help of the corporate to develop skills among the students. They must bring awareness among the students about the challenges and conduct classes or training sessions once in a week to upgrade skills among students. They must go to villages and enlighten students about the challenges arising due to skills-gap so that students take more interest to acquire the desired skills and abilities apart from knowledge that they acquire in educational institutions.

Educational institutions must shell out students who have not only qualifications but also competencies to enhance employability among their students. It requires integrated efforts from all stakeholders such as students, educators, recruiters, parents, educational institutions, and non-governmental organizations to enhance employability among students. Remember that employers look not only for qualified students but also employable and deployable students who can be productive in the workplace on the very first day to enhance their organizational excellence and effectiveness. To conclude, there has to be coordination from all sources to teach and train students effectively so that they will become employable and deployable at the corporate, and be able to lead the nation successfully.

"The biggest mistake that you can make is to believe that you are working for somebody else. Job security is gone. The driving force of a career must come from the individual. Remember: Jobs are owned by the company, you own your career!" - Earl Nightingale

Pledge: Be employable and deployable to have a foothold in the corporate world.

17

21 Timeless Tools to Become a CEO

"Being a CEO still means sitting across the table from big institutional investors and showing your leadership and having them believe in you." - Christie Hefner

When you look at Larry Page and Sergey Brin of Google, Mark Zuckerberg of Facebook, Jerry Yang & David Filo of Yahoo, Pierre Omidyar of Ebay, Matt Mullenweg of WordPress, and Chad Hurley and Steve Chen of Youtube, it is obvious that they are all CEOs who made it big during their youth. Do you also want to become a young CEO like them? Or do you want to become a CEO quickly? Then, there are a number of tools you must adopt to become a CEO. But I have condensed the key tools to save your time and ensure essence quickly. The CEO is the highest paid person in an organization who reports directly to the Board of Directors and Shareholders of the company. It is the pinnacle position and a prestigious one that every employee craves to reach. Precisely, it is the tipping point for any ambitious employee in his or her career ladder. Here are the 21 tools to reach your CEO position quickly:

1. **Develop a CEO Mindset:** It is rightly said that a battle is won twice – first in your mind and then in reality. You must think like a CEO first to become a CEO. Find out what is required to become a CEO and start acquiring the knowledge, skills, and abilities to excel as a CEO.
2. **Follow the Road Less Travelled:** When you look at Steve Jobs, he followed the road less traveled and excelled as an innovation legend. Hence, don't get into the rat race. Explore the unexplored areas where you find a huge potential and better opportunities, and then work on them.

Become a smart worker rather than a hard worker. Robert Frost rightly quoted, "Two roads diverged in a wood and I – I took the one less traveled by."

3. **Work in Line Positions than in Staff Positions:** The employees who work in line positions rather than in staff positions have better prospects of reaching the top positions quickly. Those who work in line positions work on core activities while those who work in staff positions work on supporting areas of the sector or industry they are into.
4. **Write Your Failure Resume:** It sounds strange, right? In fact, you learn more from your failures than from others as failures teach you several hard lessons and let you know what did not work for you. A failure resume helps you find your blind spots. Hence, follow the three-step process while writing your failure resume. In the first column, list out your failures; in the second column, write down why you have failed; in the third column, mention what are the lessons learned from your failures. It helps you reflect your mind and serves you during introspection. Preparing a failure resume will minimize your mistakes in future and

maximize your leadership success. Mason Cooley once said, "If you call failures experiments, you can put them in your resume and claim them as achievements."

5. **Acquire a Positive, Right and Strong Attitude:** It is your attitude that determines your altitude. Hence, you must build your attitude. At times, attitude is preferred over experience. For instance, a person with a great attitude with nil experience is preferred over a person with great experience but with nil attitude. That is the power of attitude! You must possess positive, right, and strong attitude. Positive attitude is about looking at the things from a positive perspective. Right attitude is about emphasizing the right means to achieve your outcomes. Strong attitude is about sticking to your principles through thick and thin to accomplish your goals despite the odds being stacked against you.
6. **Build Your Leadership Abilities:** Leadership is an ability anybody can acquire. It is the key component to take you to the top quickly. It differentiates between the chaff and cheese. Leadership is the ability to lead from the front by

taking responsibility, setting an example, influencing others and walking your talk. When you lead it shows your inner spark and projects your abilities and people follow you based on them. Remember that only leaders can become CEOs, not followers. Hence, build your leadership abilities.

7. **Hone Your Conceptual Skills:** Robert Katz said there are three skills needed in varied proportions at each level of management. They are technical skills, human skills, and conceptual skills. As you go from lower to middle, and to top level management, you must possess more of conceptual skills and less of technical skills while the percentage of the human skills remain constant at each level of management. The human skills can be called soft skills, and technical skills can be called hard skills. There is an equal significance attached to soft skills at each level of management but the significance for hard skills decreases when you go to senior level positions as you do more of decision making and trouble shooting at the top level. In addition, you have to provide your vision to your company. Hence, you

must hone your conceptual skills to touch your tipping point.

8. **Blend Hard and Soft Skills:** A judicious blend of both hard and soft skills is needed to reach the top. Hard skills are about your technical aspects while soft skills are about your polite and pleasing way of communicating with others. Rather soft skills are the presentation of your hard skills. It is improper to think that hard skills alone will help you get to the top. In fact, hard skills will get you to the top while soft skills will put you firmly on your corporate ladder.
9. **Emphasize more on EQ:** David Campbell, The Center for Creative Leadership unfolds, "Half of the CEOs in the world are below average." Hence, your (Emotional Quotient) EQ plays a more important role than (Intelligence Quotient) IQ. Here is good news! EQ can be acquired through various means including reading, training, observation, experience, and practice. IQ is inborn while EQ can be cultivated. Hence, develop your EQ and blend it with IQ proportionately and effectively to reach the top.

10. **Work in Teams:** When you work in teams you display your strengths and leverage others' skills. You develop tolerance to others' views and empathize with them. You also generate better results. You develop a great synergy and network that will catapult you to the top quickly. In addition, you develop emotional intelligence which is one of the key components for your leadership effectiveness.
11. **Be an Expert in Your Domain:** You must discover your strengths and talents and work on those areas only. You must focus on them forever to achieve the desired outcomes quickly. Acquire knowledge continuously in your area of interest. Reinvent yourself with the changing times and technology. Update yourself constantly by networking with the people sharing your interests, knowledge and also to know the latest developments. Create your online professional image so that people notice your brand and look for your leadership.
12. **Involve in Job Rotation:** Job rotation is about doing various tasks outside your routine nature of work. It has multiple advantages. It eliminates

boredom and keeps you active. You get to know what is happening in other areas. It helps you develop conceptual skills. Above all, it helps you stay motivated. Hence, undertake various roles and responsibilities beyond your specified nature of work within the organization to know something of everything and everything of something.

13. **Brand Yourself:** Nowadays, branding is an imperative. It is an effective tool to build your career and project your personality to others. You must be careful before branding. Choose carefully how you would like to brand yourself as your brand will enhance your professional image and longevity. You must brand based on your principles, philosophies, competencies and capabilities. Accelepoint Webzine reveals, "Even individuals need to develop a brand for themselves .... Whatever your area of expertise, you can take steps to make people think of YOU when they think of your field."
14. **Be Loyal to Your Organization:** Some employees change their jobs often for peanuts but they must know that changing their jobs too often

dents their credibility. Research reveals that most of the CEOs worked for a long period in their organizations and ultimately they reached the top. They emphasized on their careers, not jobs. When you work in an organization for a long duration, your talents will be spotted, and you will be slotted in the leadership pipeline through continuous training and development thus reaching the top quickly. In addition, most of the companies promote their senior talent for CEO position rather than hiring from outside. In fact, job hoppers took 27 years to become CEO while the loyal ones took about 23 years to become CEO. Hence, be loyal to your organization.

15. **Manage Complexity and Uncertainty:** Although technology is a boon it has become a bane in some aspects bringing a lot of uncertainty and complexity. You must develop tolerance towards complexity. You must be flexible to accommodate with open arms.
16. **Embrace Change:** The only thing constant in this world is change. Hence, change before you are forced to change. Change is painful and stressful if you view it negatively. In contrast, if

you view it positively, you will be able to embrace it with open arms and enjoy every moment. Remember the words of Charles Darwin, "It is not the strongest of the species that survives, nor the most intelligent that survives. It is the one that is the most adaptable to change."

17. **Update with Latest Technology:** Technology is changing rapidly. You must update yourself with rapidly changing technology to leverage several benefits and save your time, money and energy. In addition, most of the young CEOs are from the technology domain. If you are good at technology, and start doing research you will get more ideas thus founding a company and becoming a CEO at a young age itself.
18. **Take Feedback Regularly:** Ken Blanchard said, "Feedback is the breakfast of champions." When you take feedback you assess yourself where you stand in terms of your performance and results. If you failed to achieve your goals you will be able to spot the barriers that prevented you from reaching your goals. You can address them and move forward.

19. **Look at Similarities, not Differences:** The globe has become a small village where technology connected all people together under one platform. Develop flexibility and respect all communities. Treat diversity as an opportunity, not a challenge. Be tolerant towards other communities. Empathize with others. Love your mother but don't hate others' mothers. As your mother is precious to you, others' mothers are equally precious to them. As your community is close to your heart, others' communities are close to their heart. Hence, look at similarities and connect with others to gain acceptance and earn respect. M. Scott Peck rightly remarked, "Share our similarities, celebrate our differences."
20. **Coach Others:** When you coach others you earn their goodwill; develop rapport with them; and you excel as a true leader. Most of the employees prefer to work with superiors who handhold and coach them. They look for their career guidance and support. Hence, coach people, support them and build leaders around yourself. When you do so, you stand in a better position to scale the

corporate ladder quickly. Remember that real leaders build leaders around themselves.

21. **Learn Constantly:** Remember the sage advice of my friend and mentor, Marshall Goldsmith, the CEO Coach, *What Got You Here Won't Get You There.* You need to update yourself regularly with the latest tools and techniques to reach your next higher position. What worked to reach your present successful position might not work to reach your next higher position. Hence, acquire secrets and strategies, and update your tools and techniques to become even more successful in your professional life.

To conclude, these 21 tools help you become a CEO and achieve success quickly in your chosen sphere. Follow these time tested tools to touch your tipping point. Remember that leadership is a journey, not a destination. Hence, enjoy your journey to becoming a CEO. Good luck!

"Just because you are CEO, don't think you have landed. You must continually increase your learning, the way you think, and the way you approach the organization. I've never forgotten that." - Indra Nooyi

Pledge: Adopt 21 timeless tools to become a CEO quickly.

18

Can HR Leaders Excel as the CEOs of a Company?

"HR should not be defined by what it does but by what it delivers - results that enrich the organization's value to customers, investors and employees" - Dave Ulrich

Do you know why professionals from the teaching domain alone become the principals and deans in educational institutions? Do you know why pilots with flying experience alone become the Air Chief Marshalls in the Indian Air Force?

The answer is that they belong to core areas of organizations, and fall in the bracket of line organizations. They can comfortably handle major operations and activities as they have come from core functional areas. In contrast, the people who belong to non-core functional areas fall in the bracket of staff organizations and play a supporting role to the professionals coming from core functional areas. So is the case of HR leaders who support CEOs rather than stepping into the shoes of CEOs. They grow as kingmakers who rarely become kings. In fact, HR leaders are the backbone of any organization as they handle from recruitment to retirement and serve as the lifeblood of any organization to achieve organizational excellence and effectiveness. If you look at Mohandas Pai of Infosys Technologies Ltd of India he could not become CEO of Infosys as he is from the HR area; he subsequently put in his papers.

Studies show that 83 per cent of HR leaders don't reach the level of CEOs. Another research reveals that only 5 percent of HR directors reach the position of CEO. That means something is wrong somewhere. Either HR directors don't possess the requisite mindset to excel as CEO or they are not treated on par with other areas - finance, operations and marketing, legal, IT and strategy. In addition, HR leaders are often treated as facilitators, not value creators. They train and groom leaders to become CEOs but they cannot excel as CEOs.

Challenges for HR Leaders

It is observed that HR leaders may not demonstrate both technical and business acumen which is needed to become a CEO. There is an impression that some of the HR leaders remain like frogs in the well. If they want to step into the shoes of CEO they must develop a broad mindset with a judicious mix of soft, hard, and conceptual skills. It is unfair to blame their non-elevation to CEO level as a prejudice. The fact is that it requires a unique mindset to excel as a CEO which HR leaders often lack. Since HR leaders work in a specific area for many areas they often fail to come out it. They prefer to remain as a big fish in a small pond while the leaders from other functional areas especially with technical acumen always remain in the effective zone, and prefer to remain big fish in a big pond.

Everyone has a crucial role to play in an organization. Hence, it is ideal to do their tasks effectively rather than entering into others' territory because a leader who is successful in one area may not be successful in another area. Remember that everyone has their own competencies and capabilities. Hence, it is better to focus on their core areas to do justification and excel professionally.

What is CEO Acumen?

A CEO must change as per the situation like a chameleon. S/he must apply different strokes to different people in different situations which may not be possible for HR leaders who are experts in making people dance as per their tunes. If required, a CEO has to dance as per the tunes of other stakeholders to get the tasks executed successfully.

The CEO of the company has to be an all-rounder. S/he has to be jack of all trades and master of management and leadership. S/he must know the length and breadth of everything and depth of the core domain. It is usually possible for the executives who are from the technical domain. The CEO must be a troubleshooter, crisis manager, communicator, strategist, and above all, a visionary. The HR leaders are very strong in their core area as they handle the precious human resources. However, they lack certain technical, operational and other skills resulting in non-elevation to CEO level. At the same time, it should not become a barrier for ambitious HR leaders to become CEOs.

The personality of a CEO is different from an HR leader. Everyone has a role to perform and hence, it is better for HR leaders to work in their territory while CEOs work in their territory. If HR leaders want to grow as CEOs they must learn to take risk and thrive on uncertainty and complexity as these are the hallmarks of CEOs. They must come out of their comfort zones and develop a broad perspective about other areas to know something of everything. They are predominantly strong in people skills and human skills but are found to be deficient in technical skills.

Ground Realities

HR leaders convey the impression that they care for employees as it is their core role. Likewise, leaders of each area such as finance, operations, and sales and marketing carry the impressions as messiahs of their departments. However, the CEO carries the impression as messiah of all departments with main focus on the organizational bottom lines. This mindset makes a huge difference to achieve organizational effectiveness. Hence, leaders cutting across their areas must appreciate this fact and must come out of their core functional areas to gain overall acceptance if they are ambitious to grow as CEOs.

Acquire CEO Acumen

To become a CEO, the leader must acquire technical and business acumen; possess hard and soft skills; and apply hard and soft power. Hence, the CEO aspirant whether from HR or from non-HR background must acquire these ingredients to become a CEO. When you look at Jack Welch he became CEO of GE despite being a chemical engineer. What you need to have is the fire and ambition. It doesn't matter whether you hail from HR or non-HR background. It is only an excuse for HR to blame the system. Remember that it is the bad tradesman who blames his tools, and the wise tradesman who works from where he is; works with what he has; and executes the tasks effectively. Hence, HR leaders should not indulge in blame game about the system. They must acquire the requisite qualities and spot the opportunities to become a CEO. If they are at the entry level, it is better for them to enter into line organizations rather than into staff organizations to accomplish their ambition to become CEO in the long run. Here are the tools for HR leaders to excel as CEOs:

- The HR leaders must shed their inhibitions and declare their ambition to become CEOs to get noticed in the long run. They must aim high and learn the functions of other departments to widen their knowledge base and understand the whole picture of the organization. It broadens their conceptual skills which is much needed for HR leaders to grow as CEOs.

- They must build their CEO brand consistently through various means. If required, they must follow the concept of job rotation to excel as well-rounded professionals to become CEO.
- They must learn to manage VUCA which is the acronym for volatility, uncertainty, complexity and ambiguity. It requires tons of patience, tact and diplomacy to manage the current challenges and changes.
- They must possess strategic vision and knowledge and display the same. They must be able to integrate various verticals and departments within their mind to see the big picture.
- They must think out-of-the box to grow as CEOs as becoming CEO involves not only managing people but also various aspects of troubleshooting, decision making and being visionary.
- CEOs must be able to think laterally and must be in a position to look strategically. Hence, HR leaders must think laterally and act strategically to become CEOs.
- HR leaders must recognize that their future lies

outside the HR department. The sooner they realize that, the better for them to grow as CEOs.

- CEOs deal with various stakeholders such as governmental agencies, financial institutions, marketing, suppliers, clients and managing both internal and external environment. Hence, HR leaders must set their vision in the early stage of their careers and develop CEO mindset by learning various aspects.
- They must remember that CEOs are made, not born. Hence, they must demonstrate their passion and ambition to excel as CEOs. They must craft their vision while in the early stage of their careers and work towards this direction.

Change Your Mindset to Excel as a CEO

"The one thing I have learned as a CEO is that leadership at various levels is vastly different. When I was leading a function or a business, there were certain demands and requirements to be a leader. As you move up the organization, the requirements for leading that organization don't grow vertically; they grow exponentially." - Indra Nooyi

If you read HR books authored by Dave Ulrich, Norm Smallwood and Kate Sweetman and other HR scholars and practitioners, you will have a fair idea about the challenges of HR and the roles and responsibilities of HR leaders. The HR leaders are basically people-oriented leaders and if they want to grow to the level of CEO they must learn to become task-oriented leaders without forgetting people-orientation. In this way, they will be able to have the cake and eat it too.

There are very few CEOs with an HR background currently as HR is basically treated as a supporting role rather than a core role. To become CEO of a company it requires all-round experience. Being strong in one domain alone doesn't help. Hence, HR leaders must raise their bars and come out of their comfort zones and core domains. They must get involved in job rotation and participate in cross-functional areas including finance, production, operations, sales and marketing. They must close the gap between theory and practice. Remember that becoming CEO of a company requires a unique blend of mindset, tool set and skill set. Hence, acquire and accomplish your ambition to excel as a CEO.

"Leadership matters, because leaders are responsible for identifying and resolving the challenges of their stakeholders – customers, investors and employees. Leadership starts with better results." – Dave Ulrich and Norm Smallwood

Pledge: Acquire CEO acumen and learn the ropes of other departments to become a CEO.

19

Coach Future Leaders

"A true Master is not the one with the most students, but one who creates the most Masters. A true leader is not the one with the most followers, but one who creates the most leaders." — Neale Donald Walsch

Presently organizations are taking immense interest in providing leadership development programs to their employees as there is a dire need for building new leaders due to the retirement of Baby Boomers. When Baby boomers retire there will be a shortage of senior leaders and CEOs within the organizations. In addition, the duration of the CEOs tenure is decreasing which is a major challenge for organizations. Hence, organizations are taking keen interest to coach future leaders to enhance their excellence and effectiveness and keep their leadership pipeline seamlessly flowing with talent.

Before companies intend to build their future leaders they must identify the right talent first so that they can bank on them to meet their future needs. They must effectively engage Human Resources (HR) that deals with the people from recruitment to retirement and follows the cliché *hire for attitude and train for skills*. Hence, recruit the talent that is good at attitude and train and groom with requisite skills and abilities with a long-term perspective.

Spot the Right Talent

Here are the ways to spot the right talent for building future leaders:

- There are huge costs involved in providing leadership training programs for employees. Hence, it is desirable to spot the right material to make wise investments in training them. If companies invest in wrong talent there will be a drain in resources. Hence, companies must look at the right candidates during recruitment itself who are willing to learn and grow with a positive, right and strong attitude.
- Find out the X factor among the talent. X factor is something people have it within themselves. It is a kind of fire and passion people have and such people can contribute their best and grow quickly in their careers.

- Find out candidates' previous history - whether they contributed in teams and made any difference to their organizations. At times, past contribution is a barometer for future performance. Find out what unique strengths, skills, abilities and knowledge they possess to keep them in the pipeline for future leadership training programs.
- Check their previous performance if they are already working. Identifying their engagement to the organization and contribution through various feedback including 90 degree, 180 degree and 360 degree; this feedback helps the companies greatly in deciding whether to invest in their training.
- Spot the leadership spark and identify their inclination to leadership roles and responsibilities. Are they willing to risk and explore? Do they follow the road less travelled? Are they trendsetters? Can they accept both bouquets and brickbats equally? Do they have a heart to make a difference to the lives of others? When companies are convinced that the potential candidates have all these ingredients then the former can invest their resources on the latter with a long-term perspective.

Timeless Tools to Coach Future Leaders

After spotting the right talent the companies must provide leadership development programs and coach the candidates constantly to enhance productivity and performance and also keep such precious talent on the leadership pipeline with a long view. There are a number of tools to coach future leaders but some of them have been covered in one of the chapters titled, '21 Timeless Tools to Become a CEO' in this book. Here are some tools to coach future leaders:

1. **Set a Broad Vision:** Winston Churchill once said, "If you are doing big things, you attract big men. If you are doing the little things, you attract little men. Little men usually cause trouble." Broad vision helps come out of the comfort zone constantly thus getting the best out of the talent. It helps them set short-term, long-term and life-long goals. It helps align these three set of goals regularly and enhances focus thus providing meaning to their personal, professional and social lives.

2. **Build a Global Mindset:** The globe has become a small village due to the rapid growth in technology. It is well connected and we can get to know everything at the click of a mouse. It is essential to develop a broad mindset by understanding various cultures by looking at similarities and ignoring differences.
3. **Manage Time:** God gifted all of us with 24 hours and we must know how to manage it effectively by prioritizing and following it meticulously. Enlighten employees with Pareto's Principle of 80: 20 and train them to make use of their time on productive activities by identifying and eliminating the time wasters.
4. **Delegate the Routine Tasks:** The superiors must delegate their routine tasks to their subordinates so that they can save their time and gradually engage their subordinates to take on more responsibilities. It infuses confidence among the subordinates and builds leadership abilities and skills.
5. **Encourage Risk-taking:** Risk is an integral element of leadership. It is an inherent element in everyday life. A ship is safe when it is in harbor but it is not meant for that. God gifted us life to

explore and experiment. Hence, we must learn to take risk and explore to make it big. Remember, not to take a risk is also a risk.

6. **Empower them:** When superiors empower their subordinates the latter come out of their comfort zones; overcome their apprehensions and explore various avenues to lead from the front. They will be able to make decisions, and experiment thus building their competencies and capabilities. Sometimes subordinates may surprise their superiors by coming out with innovative ideas and outcomes thus adding value to organizations.
7. **Provide Feedback Constantly:** Ken Blanchard rightly said that feedback is the breakfast of champions. When superiors provide feedback to their subordinates regularly the latter can identify their strong and weak areas thus overcoming their weaknesses gradually and growing as leaders rapidly. While giving feedback make sure that it is behavior-centric, not individual-centric. Provide sandwich feedback preferably. Sandwich feedback starts with a positive compliment; ends with a positive praise; and embeds the negative comments that are aimed at bringing out the desired behavioral improvement.

8. **Enhance EQ:** Emotional intelligence quotient (EQ) is gaining importance as it is the major ingredient of leadership. It can be acquired through teaching and training programs and developed through practice. EQ can be defined as a five-fold process of identifying your own emotions, managing your own emotions, identifying the emotions of the individuals around you, managing their emotions and motivating them to lead from the front. Hence, coaches and trainers must emphasize and equip EQ among the future leaders.
9. **Engage Passionate Senior Leaders:** Fred A. Manske, Jr. said, "The ultimate leader is not afraid to develop people to the point they surpass him or her in knowledge and ability." Jack Welch conducted leadership training programs to train and groom budding leaders in GE. It helped him grasp the challenges at the ground level and also inspired budding talent to understand the challenges at the higher level. In addition, it encouraged the talent to dream and achieve big like Jack Welch.

10. **Build *Level 5 Leaders*:** It is a fact that leaders build leaders and we need *Level 5 Leaders* to build future leaders. Jim Collins highlighted *Level 5 Leaders* in his book, *Good to Great.* The *Level 5 Leaders* are a paradoxical blend of personal humility and professional will. They are passionate leaders who don't mind when others take credit for their contribution. They want to make a difference in the lives of others. Hence, spotting senior leaders who are *Level 5 Leaders* and deploying them to build future *Level 5 Leaders* helps greatly to organizations.
11. **Create Collaborative rather than Competitive Attitude:** In the current global business environment, it is essential to compete and collaborate as per the situation. People often have the attitude to compete which is human nature. But those who want to excel as leaders must develop a collaborative attitude to get the best for them and their organizations. Above all, collaboration helps in eliminating ill-will among the members and leveraging their strengths.

12. **Inculcate Business Acumen:** Most of the talent often comes with technical acumen learning either from the educational institutions or in the workplace. They must also learn about business acumen which is more important to excel as leaders. It mostly comes with experience and by undertaking challenging roles and responsibilities.
13. **Learn from Failures:** The Poet, Archibald MacLeish quoted, "There is only one thing more painful than learning from experience, and that is not learning from experience." Read good books and learn from their experiences to avoid mistakes and enhance your leadership effectiveness. It is rightly said that a wise person learns from the mistakes of others whereas the foolish person learns from own experience. Hence, be a wise person by learning from the failures of others to enhance your leadership effectiveness and success.
14. **Enlighten that Leadership is not a Popularity Contest:** It is not easy to please all. The path to leadership is not a cakewalk. It requires blending IQ with EQ; taking bouquets and brickbats equally; spreading the fame during successes and taking the blame during failures; and above all,

being competitive and collaborative as per the situation.

15. **Remember *'What Got You Here, Won't Get You There'*:** Marshall Goldsmith in his book, *What Got You Here, Won't Get You There—How Successful People, Become Even More Successful!* reveals that you need to learn continuously, take feedback regularly, and identify the barriers to reach your next higher level. What worked to get you to this position might not work to reach you to your next higher position as the times and technologies; and tools and techniques are changing rapidly. Hence, learn continuously, and acquire new tools and techniques constantly to update, innovate and excel as a great leader.

Recession is an opportunity for organizations to train and groom talent because during the upturn they don't find time to concentrate on leadership development programs as they are busy with improving the bottom lines and adding value to customers and clients. Hence, organizations must treat recession as an opportunity rather than a threat to retain talent and train them for future needs.

Encourage coaching and avoid poaching. It is better to coach and groom the leaders to readiness rather than to poach when needed. Poaching resolves problems temporarily but coaching resolves problems permanently and enhances employee engagement and ensures employee loyalty. An engaged employee is always an asset to any organization. Hence, adopt these tools to coach future leaders to achieve organizational excellence and effectiveness.

"The final test of a leader is that he leaves behind in other people the convictions and will to carry on." - Walter Lippman

Pledge: Spot the right talent and build the leaders around you.

20

What would I Like to be Remembered For?

"Educationists should build the capacities of the spirit of inquiry, creativity, entrepreneurial and moral leadership among students and become their role model." - A P J Abdul Kalam

A.P.J. Kalam – An Inspiration for Students

I attended the speech delivered by the former President of India, Dr. APJ Kalam on March 29, 2013. I was very

impressed with his charisma, and his ability to connect with the youth through his magical words and effective messages to achieve success with integrity.

Many students might ask me the question – "Is it possible to achieve success with integrity?" Yes. It is possible. But it takes several years of a journey filled with struggles and sacrifices. Currently some of the Indian youth want success at any cost. But the reality is that it takes tons of efforts to achieve success. If people adopt shortcuts to achieve success they fail at the end miserably. If people achieve success due to luck they cannot sustain it when the luck runs out. If people focus on hard work, smart work, wise work and ethical work they will be able to achieve lasting success that is well emulated by all people in the world. We take Swami Vivekananda as a symbol of success and as a youth icon because he practiced what he preached. He emphasized on means, not ends. He emphasized on ethical means to convey the right message to the youth and the world. He was one of the Indians who put India on the global map by highlighting India's unity in diversity and promoting fraternity and universal brotherhood in the Chicago Conference.

Therefore, you must set a vision based on your values, and talents and build skills around them. You must emphasize on ethical means to achieve success with integrity. You must be willing to wait for results. If you don't find results take corrective steps and move forward to achieving lasting success with integrity. Above all, develop a great attitude to serve your society, country and the world as a whole to ensure lasting happiness and peace everywhere.

Kalam implored the youth to write down 'what would I like to be remembered for' in the speech. Here is a detailed blueprint to proceed forward:

What would I Like to be Remembered for?

"An individual should have an aim for 20 years ahead. He or she should focus on acquiring knowledge continuously and work hard towards achieving the aim and persevere to overcome all problems."- APJ Abdul Kalam

Everyday many people are born and dead. How many of them leave a mark for others to follow? How many of them will be remembered soon after their death? It is a few people, right! We remember a few Indian personalities like

Swami Vivekananda, Mahatma Gandhi and Subhas Chandra Bose. But we don't remember many people who lived in the past. It is because some leaders are legends who lived beyond their times with their unique contributions to society and mankind. Do you also want to be remembered like them or leave this world like any other insignificant individual? If you want to be remembered beyond your lifetime you must set goals and serve others. We must remember that God gave us one life and we must do everything in one life only. Hence, you must create a blueprint - "What would I like to be remembered for" today itself to stand out from others to soar like an eagle.

How to Become a Legend?

To become a legend, you must inspire people with what you have and by giving what they want. You will be remembered beyond your lifetime. Find out the strengths you have, and the needs of the people around you and beyond your times. Acquire the requisite attitude, skills and knowledge and share them with others. Reprogram your mind through the mirroring technique. Give positive commands. Visualize yourself that you are a legend. You become the way you think. Ralph Waldo Emerson quoted,

"We become what we think about all day long." Hence, think round the clock that you are a legend and born to do something for others. Take initiative. Take the common causes that are neglected by others but need to be addressed immediately. Influence the people around, build teams, motivate them and achieve the objectives successfully. You will become a legend. Remember that legends are not born, but made. Here are 12 steps to follow to create your blueprint to become a legend during your lifetime:

12 Steps to Become a Legend

1. Identify how you would like to be remembered. Would you like to be remembered as a great scientist, educator, cricketer, actor, leader or someone with a big heart to make a difference in the lives of others?
2. After developing clarity, spot your passions and consider your age, opportunities, and availability of resources.
3. Shortlist the passion which you can pursue based on your strengths and build skills around it.
4. Invest some time regularly to achieve it.

5. Manage external distractions to ensure that you stay focused on your passions and goals.
6. Build a network of friends and followers who respect and appreciate your principles and philosophies and ideas and ideologies.
7. Read relevant books in your area of interest.
8. Take someone as a role model. For instance, Plato took Socrates; Aristotle took Plato; and Alexander took Aristotle as their role models and reached great heights. Also, Swami Vivekananda took Ramakrishna Paramahamsa as his role model and mentor.
9. Develop the attitude of gratitude and make others feel important.
10. Become a servant leader with more emphasis on people-orientation rather than on task-orientation.
11. Reflect your thoughts regularly and renew yourself physically, emotionally, mentally and spiritually.
12. Contribute your best without expecting anything from others because what goes around comes around.

Conclusion

Be clear about what you want to become in your personal, professional and social life after 20 years of your life from now, and how you would like to be remembered in your lifetime. Create a vision on three levels – personal, professional and social levels accordingly. It must be the most important page in your life. Articulate your vision effectively through stories to strike a chord with others to achieve the desired outcomes. Above all, work with integrity and wisdom with a true heart to make a difference in the lives of others. You will become a living legend and you will be remembered beyond your lifetime.

"My message, especially to young people is to have courage to think differently, courage to invent, to travel the unexplored path, courage to discover the impossible and to conquer the problems and succeed. These are great qualities that they must work towards. This is my message to the young people." - Abdul Kalam

Pledge: Achieve success with integrity.

Oath for the Youth[1]

1. I will have a goal and work hard to achieve that goal. I realize that small aim is a crime.

2. I will work with integrity and succeed with integrity.

3. I will be a good member of my family, a good member of the society, a good member of the nation and a good member of the world.

4. I will always try to save or better someone's life, without any discrimination of caste, creed, language religion or state. Wherever I am, a thought will always come to my mind. That is "What can I give?"

5. I will always protect and enhance the dignity of every human life without any bias.

6. I will always remember the importance of time. My motto will be "Let not my winged days, be spent in vain".

7. I will always work for clean home, clean planet Earth and clean energy.

---

[1] www.abdulkalam.com

8. As a youth of my nation, I will work and work with courage to achieve success in all my tasks and enjoy the success of others.

9. I am as young as my faith and as old as my doubt. Hence, I will light up then, the lamp of faith in my heart.

10. My National Flag flies in my heart and I will bring glory to my nation.

By, Dr. APJ Abdulkalam
www.abdulkalam.com

Reference

www.abdulkalam.com

Acknowledgement

The author thanks the former President of India, Dr. A.P.J. Kalam for giving the permission to incorporate his pledge in this chapter.

21

Professor M.S.Rao's Message to Indian Students

Dear Leaders,

It is an honor to share some thoughts with my students who constitute the majority of the Indian population. You are the force of India! You are the power of India! You are the leaders of this great country! Many revolutions are successful with your support. You have transformed the Indian society extraordinarily. Because you think what is possible. You think what is feasible. You make things happen. And you see that India becomes prosperous.

Around 2000 years ago, India was the leader in the world. Long ago, we had the greatest civilization on the earth.

We were one of the richest countries in the world. We had great leaders like Ashoka who ruled not only India but some parts of Asia. Where do we stand now? We are at the crossroads of Indian history.

66 years ago, we got independence from the British. When we look back what did we achieve? Let us ask ourselves honestly. It is time to take stock of the situation. It is unfortunate that India still lives in poverty and malnutrition. We have several challenges currently. The major one is corruption which has become a cancer to our Indian society. It is very sad to note that corruption entered into all areas of the Indian system. Remember, the day corruption enters into educational institutions and the armed forces, the country will collapse like a house of cards. Therefore, you must strive for a society which is free from corruption. That is the need of the hour indeed!

India has 28 states and 7 union territories. India is a country of contrasts in many aspects. India has 22 official languages and Indians speak over 1600 dialects. India is a land of unity in diversity. We are identified through different cultures and communities but connected by a single common thread – Indianness. India is indeed incredible!

India is a great country where a minority Sikh is the Prime Minister of this great country; minority Muslims became the presidents of this great country; a Dalit leader like Dr. Ambedkar could rise and wrote the Indian constitution that protects the rights of all Indian citizens. Indian land provides ample of equal opportunities to all citizens irrespective of their region, religion, language, caste, creed and community. We are the large hearted people in the world. Eulogizing India, Roman Scholar, Romain Rolland once remarked, "If there is one place on the face of earth where all the dreams of living men have found a home from the very earliest days when man began the dream of existence, it is India."

We Indians are known for hospitality. We welcome all communities and cultures with open arms. We have a great heart to accept and accommodate anybody and everybody on the earth. That is the greatness of India! Our Indian soil is rich with diversified cultures and is highly sacred with religious tolerance and secularism. You must be proud that you are born on this great Indian soil.

India has sheltered many religions, cultures and communities. It is the land of all religions and nations on the earth. We belong to a country that taught the world about non-violence and Satyagraha. We belong to a country that taught the world about tolerance and secularism. We belong to a country that taught the world about fraternity and universal brotherhood. It was Swami Vivekananda who put India's greatness on the global map in the Chicago Conference. He conquered America without any bullet.

India is not an emerging country. It has already emerged as a great country in the world. India is the origin of 'zero' and India is the origin of the Information Age. Albert Einstein once remarked, "We owe a lot to the Indians, who taught us how to count, without which no worthwhile scientific discovery could have been made."

Indian civilization is one of the oldest surviving civilizations in the world. Mark Twain rightly remarked, "India is, the cradle of the human race, the birthplace of human speech, the mother of history, the grandmother of legend, and the great grandmother of tradition. Our most valuable and most instructive materials in the history of man are treasured up in India only."

We have the largest speaking English population in the world. We are the largest surviving democracy in the world. We have championed the self-determination of people from Asia to Africa. We are the global leader to support democratic movements across the world. We are the number one in many areas. . We are the trendsetters, not trend followers. That is the greatness of India! We are the leading contributor to the United Nations peacekeeping missions. We are preparing to take our seat on the United Nations Security Council very soon. It is time to capitalize what we have, and move on aggressively to make a mark globally.

We had great leaders like Netaji Subhash Chandra Bose, Mahatma Gandhi, and Bhagat Singh. Netaji Subhash Chandra Bose was a great patriot, a visionary leader, and an orator, who founded the Indian National Army. There are five followers of Mahatma Gandhi who bagged Nobel Prizes – Martin Luther King Jr, Nelson Mandela, Aung San Sui Ki, Dalai Lama and Barrack Obama. There are a huge number of followers for Mahatma Gandhi across the world. Our ideas and ideals are followed by great countries and great people across the world. That shows our strength! And we must make sure that Mahatma Gandhi's ideals and ideas are emulated by everyone within

India to make our country stronger and greater in the world.

We are proud to have a strong judiciary in India. We are proud to have a strong media that checks everything. Thanks to the media that it highlights any irregularities and brings corruption into the public attention.

India is successful in the Green Revolution that fed millions of Indians. We have withstood the recent recession. Many great countries and developed countries like US and UK have been hit hard due to recession. But we are not hit hard due to our strong inherent systems. It is said that if America catches cold the world sneezes. The world may sneeze, not India and Indians.

The global equations are changing rapidly. Now it is our time. A BRIC Report says that India has an important role to play in the years to come – BRIC is the acronym for Brazil, Russia, India and China. India has several strategic competitive advantages over these three countries and especially over China as India's population is young and the Chinese population is old. However, let us not rest on our laurels. It is time for us to work hard and work smart to take India forward economically.

Presently Indians are going to America to work. We Indians don't have to work anymore under Americans and foreigners. The day is not far away where Americans and foreigners will come to India and work under Indians. We will show the world what we are! We will show the world the might of India!

Let us be duty-oriented rather than rights-oriented. Let us not ask what the country has given us. Let us ask ourselves what we are giving back to our country. There must be change in the attitude of the people. There must be change in the mindset of the people.

We will work together. We will walk together. We must make a pledge that we will make India a developed country very soon. We will make India a Super Power on the earth. We will never rest until we accomplish our goal.

We had seen enough failures, separations and humiliations at the hands of foreigners. Enough is enough! Let us look back, learn lessons and move forward with confidence and optimism. It is time for India to be established internationally.

We will protect our independence by all means. We are Indians first and Indians last. No power under the sun on the earth can separate us. We are one. We will live together and we will die together. We will protect our independence by all means. We will put our motherland on the top of the world. It is our time to raise our voice and to stand out as the number one country in the world.

We will walk as brothers and sisters. We will share both sorrow and joy. We will share both pain and pleasure. If India is to be a great nation we must stand united ignoring the differences. We should stay united by looking at the commonalities. It is our time to establish ourselves internationally. We will not rest until we become a Super Power. We will bring back the lost glory. We will see to it that we become the number one nation in the world.

Be disciplined. Be tolerant towards others. Empathize with others. Respect all communities. Love your mother, but don't hate another person's mother. Remember, as your mother is precious to you, another person's mother is equally precious to him/her.

The sky is the limit for you! You have abundant opportunities currently. You are born in the right time of

Indian history. You have great potential and powers to take on this world. Bharat Mata is calling you. Develop a positive, right and strong attitude. Shoulder the responsibilities. Lead India and lead the world.

Thank you, God bless India. Jai Hind!

By, Professor M.S. Rao
http://www.facebook.com/pages/Professor-MSRao/451516514937414?skip_nax_wizard=true
http://speakermix.com/professor-m-s-rao
http://professormsraoguru.blogspot.com
http://professormsrao.blogspot.com
http://profmsr.blogspot.com

Pledge: Be proud of being an Indian.

"When I asked God for strength, He gave me difficult situations to face. When I asked God for brain and brawn, He gave me puzzles in life to solve. When I asked God for happiness, He showed me some unhappy people. When I asked God for wealth, He showed me how to work hard. When I asked God for favors, He showed me opportunities to work hard. When I asked God for peace, He showed me how to help others. God Gave me nothing

I wanted, He gave me everything I needed." – Swami Vivekananda

Appendix A

Be Optimistic Like Obama and Be a Leader Like Lincoln

"You have worked hard to live up to that great hope and trust placed in you by the American public." – Dalai Lama

The world is excited to hear the victory of American President, Barack Obama. It shows the trust and

confidence Obama enjoys in the hearts of Americans. His victory raised aspirations among the ordinary citizens and minorities that an ordinary person and especially a black can aspire and occupy the highest office in America. It also indicates the true heart of Americans who welcome all communities in their fold with magnanimity. Zindzi Mandela, the daughter of Nelson Mandela said, "I think that the symbolism of having a black man occupy the highest office is something that can make my children very aspirational to know that this is possible, you know, in their lifetime."

Obama secured a narrow majority in the popular vote as well as a wide majority of electoral votes. He made it happen despite several odds stacked against him. Obama's first win was due to the change the Americans craved for as they were against Bush and his miscalculations in Iraq. However, the second win was due to the hope he raised among the Americans despite being in turbulent times. Here are the reasons for his victory:

Obama's Branding and Leading

Obama branded himself as messiah of middle class people due to his humble origins. He made use of social media effectively to position and brand himself. His wife Michelle Obama and two daughters Malia and Sasha stood by him, and he publicly admitted it. He built a successful team around himself and aggressively campaigned to ensure his victory. This is all about his branding. When we talk about his leadership achievements, he successfully eliminated Osama, ensured pull-out of American forces from Iraq, and handled the Libyan issue effectively. He enhanced employment in America; built consumer confidence; and improved the housing market. He took the reins of a sinking American economic ship from his predecessor – Bush, and kept it floating although he could not sail it smoothly to the shore. Americans have voted him again with a hope that he would sail the American economic ship successfully to the shore.

Respect People's Verdict

Obama's win also shows that Americans don't want to change the President in order to let the change happen smoothly. In addition, Americans are aware that it would take four more years to recover from the challenges. Obama doesn't have any magic wand to address all the challenges within a span of four years. Hence, Americans voted him again so that Obama can deliver the goods effectively. Above all, in democracy, it is the people who are the Gods as they select the leaders and decide the destiny of the nation. Hence, let us respect the people's choice.

Challenges Ahead

Presently Obama has a number of challenges ahead. He must be careful during his second term as some of the second term Presidents could not do well and ended up in a fiasco. Hence, it is more challenging for Obama to live up to the rising expectations of Americans. Despite a decline in the employment problem there is still some amount of employment; roughly 3.6 million Americans are without work for a year or more and are still looking for jobs. Approximately 20 percent of the people in the age bracket of 25 to 54 don't have jobs in America. Hence, Americans want him to enhance employment opportunities; check recession; and revive the American economy. The global citizens want him to bridge the gap between the developed and the developing countries. They want him to address global warming and ensure ecological balance. They want him to check global terrorism to ensure a peaceful and tolerant world.

Make a Difference

Obama has nothing to lose as there is no third term for him. He has to be assertive in addressing various issues to make America and the world a better place to live. He has four years at his disposal to deliver the goods. Since he won with a thin margin, he should take feedback and act aggressively to address several challenges at home and overseas. He has to pull up his socks to make a positive difference from now onwards. He must walk his talk. He must emphasize less on rhetoric and more on performance. He must convert his charisma into performance and translate his vision into results. Above all, he must make a difference in the lives of global citizens.

Usage of Media by American Presidents

speech writers and gifted orators who have magical powers to move the audiences. They were born in poverty and raised by women other than their mothers; Lincoln was raised by his stepmother and Obama by his grandmother. Lincoln's mother died when Lincoln was a child while Obama's father left when Obama was a child. They accept criticism politely and take feedback for their improvement. The differences between Lincoln and Obama were that the former was a Republican while the latter is a Democrat; the former had little formal education while the latter has a good education in law.

Be Optimistic like Obama and Be a Leader like Lincoln

Barack Obama is a symbol of hope and optimism who rose from humble origins and showed to the world that everything is possible in the world. His optimism persuaded the Americans to win the second term although there were doubts about his victory. Abraham Lincoln also rose from humble origins and underwent a lot of failures during his lifetime and ultimately became the first Republican President and 16th President of America. He led from the front by managing two challenging issues such as unification of America and emancipation of slavery in America. And he succeeded as a leader. That is the reason most of the Americans look back to Lincoln for lessons whenever they faced leadership challenges. Hence, be optimist like Obama and be a leader like Lincoln to have the cake and eat it too to achieve all-round success.

Abraham Lincoln's Ten "Cannots[1]"

"You cannot bring about prosperity by discouraging thrift."

"You cannot help small men by tearing down big men.

"You cannot strengthen the weak by weakening the strong.

"You cannot lift the wage earner by pulling down the wage payer.

"You cannot help the poor man by destroying the rich.

"You cannot keep out of trouble by spending more than your income.

"You cannot further the brotherhood of man by inciting class hatred.

---

[1] http://www.illinoishistory.gov/facsimiles.htm accessed as on November 22, 2012

"You cannot establish security on borrowed money.

You cannot build character and courage by taking away man's initiative and independence.

"You cannot help men permanently by doing for them what they could and should do for themselves."

References

http://edition.presstv.ir/detail/127534.html

http://www.illinoishistory.gov/facsimiles.htm

Appendix B

Leadership Lessons from Lincoln

"Government of the people, by the people, for the people, shall not perish from the Earth." - Abraham Lincoln

Abraham Lincoln

I saw Steven Spielberg's movie *Lincoln* with great interest in India. It is a biographical movie conveying the last years of Lincoln's life handling the American Civil War including his assassination. It is based on Doris Kearns Goodwin's book *Team of Rivals: The Political Genius of Abraham Lincoln.* Here are the lessons leaders can learn from the legendary Lincoln:

- **Spread Fame and Take Blame:** Lincoln took responsibility for his mistakes and took the blame for his team's mistakes. He spread fame whenever the team achieved the desired objectives. It made Lincoln stand out from other leaders.
- **Be a Good Listener:** A good listener learns many things and can put across his ideas and insights effectively. Lincoln was a great listener, and it helped him negotiate with others effectively. Remember, all leaders are great listeners and Stephen R. Covey outlined it in his book *The Seven Habits of Highly Effective People* as follows: *seek first to understand, to be understood.*
- **Be Assertive:** Lincoln believed in assertive leadership with a win-win attitude. He was flexible but never compromised with his core principles and philosophy. When one of the Lincoln's allies told him that he cannot get the votes to pass the 13th Amendment to end slavery he asserted, "I am clothed in immense power - you will procure me these votes."

- **Blend Your Hard and Soft Skills:** Lincoln was a judicious mix of both hard and soft skills. He had great knowledge of law and the psychology of the people and knew how to articulate it effectively to achieve the desired outcomes.
- **Be Tactful:** Lincoln was argumentative as he hailed from a legal background. He used his legal background effectively and won his political rivals with ease.
- **Have a Sense of Humor:** Lincoln had a good sense of humor. Being good at humor breaks the monotony and refreshes the tense mind and connects with others quickly. The other person understands your viewpoint and gets convinced with your ideas and insights.
- **Be a Tale Teller:** Lincoln had the gift of story-telling. Telling stories is an effective way of reaching out to others. Most of the people are poor or average listeners. Hence, stories will help others visualize the situation and connect the reel content with real life events.
- **Stay Cool, Calm and Composed:** Lincoln was a charismatic leader who maintained a cool demeanor despite being provoked by his opponents. In fact, good leaders don't get

provoked in tense situations. They think through and weigh all options before making a decision. Above all, they make decisions based on their head, heart and gut.

- **Walk Your Talk:** People respect the leaders who deliver goods rather than rhetoric. During the American Civil War Lincoln walked his talk and met the wounded soldiers to build their confidence.
- **Make Friends out of Foes:** Remember that there are no permanent friends and foes in life as equations change from time to time. Lincoln inducted his political and personal rivals in his team and led America during the darkest hours of its history. He rightly quoted, "I destroy my enemies when I make them my friends."
- **Build a Strong Team:** Choose the people based on their competencies and capabilities to execute the tasks effectively. Don't bother about your personal preferences as it is always the institution and goals that are important, not your personal rivalry with others. Additionally, such a gesture elevates your image as a leader.
- **Empower People:** Lincoln empowered his General, General Ulysses S. Grant during the Civil

War and implored him to do what was right and advised him to seek assistance, if needed. Hence, empowerment gets effective outcomes.

- **Collaborate with Others:** Lincoln believed in collaboration rather than competition. He was transparent with his political opponents and worked with them to achieve his political objectives.
- **Emphasize on Ends:** Lincoln emphasized on ends and adopted various leadership tools and tactics to end slavery in America. He was idealistic as it was obvious to end slavery, even at the cost of delaying ending the war. Lincoln's idealism stands out from other American presidents thus making him a legend.
- **Do Your Duty Sincerely:** Lincoln worked under lots of complexity and uncertainty where there seemed to be no light at the end of the tunnel. But he was optimistic that war would end and slavery would be abolished. He often worked late nights and set an example for others to follow.
- **Take Feedback Regularly:** Lincoln encountered tons of trials and tribulations since childhood; he also encountered several failures. He took

feedback and improved his leadership abilities and skills constantly.

- **Be a *Level 5 Leader*:** Jim Collins in his book *Good to Great* outlined *Level 5 Leader* as one who has a paradoxical blend of personal humility and professional will. Lincoln was humble at the core and did not care who took credit for his leadership success.

The biggest lesson we can learn from Lincoln is that everything is possible in this world if there is passion and will to make a difference in the lives of people. Lincoln's greatest strength was that he worked with what he had rather than blaming circumstances. He worked under several constraints and limitations. He faced stiff opposition from his wife, staff and team members. He worked under several pressures and sacrificed all his pleasures. He worked when odds were stacked against him. He displayed tenacity and resilience. He demonstrated impeccable integrity and character although when he was losing in his life.

Lincoln was not well-educated, but well-learned. He was an exceptional American leader who was fit into history when America demanded a leader of such stature. He achieved the twin objectives of putting an end to slavery and maintaining the unity of America. Americans are treated equally and America is united as a great nation and a world's super power today; the seed for this was sown by Abraham Lincoln. Hence, I salute this American legend for his exemplary and extraordinary leadership for making a difference to American society.

"In the end, it's not the years in your life that count. It's the life in your years." - Abraham Lincoln

Appendix C

Mahatma Gandhi – A Soft Leader

"Christ gave us the goals and Mahatma Gandhi the tactics." – Dr. Martin Luther King Jr.

I led a webinar on "Soft Leadership: A New Leadership Perspective" organized by International Leadership Association on August 29, 2012. When I explained my new leadership concept - soft leadership, and the soft leaders who must contain 11 C's one of the participants asked a question, "Is there any leader in the world who possesses all C's?" I replied, "Yes, there was one leader who had all the 11C's such as character, charisma, conscience, conviction, courage, communication, compassion, commitment, consistency, consideration, and contribution - that was Mahatma Gandhi. He shook the mighty British Empire and got independence for India through truth and non-violence. He said, "In a gentle way, you can shake the world." He proved that a leader can achieve everything through moral power, soft power, soft tactics, and soft skills. He showed that it is not the size but strength that matters. It is not the physical strength but moral strength that counts. Mahatma Gandhi influenced the world through his soft leadership including five Nobel Laureates – Dr. Martin Luther King Jr, Nelson Mandela, Dalai Lama, Aung San Suu Kyi, and Barack Obama.

What is Soft Leadership?

Soft leadership is a new direction to leadership coined by me. We need this style with the changing times and technologies and due to the dynamic global business environment. This new leadership perspective is essential to meet the rising expectations of all stakeholders globally. Soft leadership can be defined as the process of setting goals; influencing people through persuasion; building strong teams; negotiating them with a win-win attitude; respecting their failures; handholding them; motivating them constantly; aligning their energies and efforts; recognizing and appreciating their contribution in accomplishing the organizational objectives with an emphasis on soft skills. It is based on the right mindset, skill set, and toolset.

Soft Leaders and 11 Characteristics

Soft leaders are the leaders who make a difference in the lives of their partners. They don't believe in leadership and followership, but in partnership. They blend hard and soft skills and lead from the front with 11 characteristics. They adopt various tools such as participation, persuasion, influence, negotiation, motivation, recognition, appreciation, and collaboration. They adopt soft power, soft tactics, and soft tools and techniques to get the tasks executed successfully. They are more of people-orientation rather than task-orientation, and adopt transformational style rather than transactional style. Precisely, soft leaders are relationship-oriented, people-orientated, service-oriented, transformational, authentic, and thought leaders who lead through soft skills. Here are the 11 characteristics that substantiate that Mahatma Gandhi was a great soft leader:

Character

Character is one of the key components of soft leaders. It is through their strong character they lead their people by influencing and guiding them. Character is the key thing that differentiates good leaders from others. In fact, good character makes a person a great leader. What counts at the end of the day in your life is who you are, not what you have. Mahatma Gandhi was a great example for character who practiced what he preached. He walked his talk throughout his life. He enlightened, "The Roots of Violence: Wealth without work, Pleasure without conscience, Knowledge without character, Commerce without morality, Science without humanity, Worship without sacrifice, Politics without principles"

Charisma

Mahatma Gandhi differentiated, "Power is of two kinds. One is obtained by the fear of punishment and the other by acts of love. Power based on love is a thousand times more effective and permanent than the one derived from fear of punishment." One of the greatest characteristics of soft leaders is their charisma. Charisma helps in connecting with others easily as people feel valued and pleased to talk with these leaders. Mahatma was a charismatic leader. He succeeded as a soft leader because of his ability to control mystical inner power. He connected with the common man with his charisma. He strongly believed, "An ounce of practice is worth more than tons of preaching."

Conscience

Conscience is one of the major key components of soft leaders as clear conscience makes them stand out from other leaders. People expect leaders to be ethical and responsible. They also look up to leaders whose conscience cares them. Conscience differentiates the right from the wrong. Leaders must have a clear conscience to convince themselves so that they can persuade others. If there is a chasm between the word and the deed, conscience reminds the same. Mahatma Gandhi was always clear with his conscience. He unveiled the mistakes he made in his autography – "Gandhi An Autobiography:

The Story of My Experiments With Truth". Every person makes mistakes but how many unveil and admit them? In fact, it requires a lot of courage to reveal one's wrong-doings. He rightly said, "The human voice can never reach the distance that is covered by the still small voice of conscience."

Conviction

Mahatma Gandhi asserted, "You can chain me, you can torture me, you can even destroy this body, but you will never imprison my mind." Conviction is another key ingredient for soft leadership without which the soft leaders cannot lead successfully. It is their convictions that take soft leaders forward and inspire their people to move forward toward achieving their goals. Mahatma Gandhi was a symbol of sacrifice and convictions. He said, "A 'No' uttered from the deepest conviction is better than a 'Yes' merely uttered to please, or worse, to avoid trouble." During India's independence he was subjected to several hardships but he strongly believed in his convictions. Hence, Mahatma Gandhi was an apt example for conviction.

Courage

Mahatma Gandhi said, "The weak can never forgive. Forgiveness is the attribute of the strong." Courage is an integral part of soft leadership. Courage doesn't mean fighting with others physically. Courage means standing for your principles and policies, and values and ethics. Mahatma Gandhi remarked, "Strength does not come from physical capacity. It comes from an indomitable will." He stood for his values of non-violence and Satyagraha. Remember what counts at the end of the day is neither your muscle power nor money power but your moral power. Hence, Mahatma Gandhi was a great example for courageous leadership and soft leadership.

Communication

Leaders express their ideas, ideals, and insights and persuade others to follow them through communication skills. And soft leaders adopt assertive communication. Assertive communication is the ability to communicate firmly but politely. Mahatma Gandhi was a great communicator who never compromised with his principles but expressed them politely and adopted them firmly. He communicated with the people through practice and by setting an example. He communicated in the language the people understood and not in the language he knew. He said, "I have nothing new to teach the world. Truth and Non-violence are as old as the hills. All I have done is to try experiments in both on as vast a scale as I could."

Compassion

When we refer to compassion, two leaders flash in our minds – Mahatma Gandhi and Mother Teresa. Mahatma Gandhi was a compassionate leader whose heart was filled with tons of compassion. He empathized with the people of all religions and faiths and respected them. He was an empathic leader who had the ability to step into the shoes of others and understand the things from others' perspective. Once he was travelling in a train, and he was standing at the door enjoying the beautiful scenery of India. One of his chappals slipped away and fell down from the train. He threw the other chappal as well so that the finder can benefit as he would have a pair instead of just one chappal. Keeping one chappal with him would be of no use to him or the finder. It shows his empathy and compassion. Mahatma Gandhi moved with untouchables and gave them due respect. He said, "Compassion is a muscle that gets stronger with use." Compassion is an integral characteristic of soft leadership. In fact, compassion differentiates soft leaders from other leaders. It helps connect with others easily. People appreciate the leaders who care and touch them.

Commitment

Commitment is the key characteristic of soft leaders. Mahatma Gandhi was committed to truth, non-violence, and peace. He rightly remarked, "My commitment is to truth not consistency." He believed in simplicity and humility. He was committed to fight against inequality and injustice when he was in South Africa and India. He was committed to fight against suppression and oppression. He was committed to Hindu-Muslim unity. He once remarked, "I don't have a message. My message is my life." His commitment to the cause of India's freedom was firm. As a result, he made a significant difference in the lives of Indians.

Consistency

Consistency is another important ingredient for soft leadership. Leaders need to demonstrate their consistency so as to have a profound impact on their people. People expect leaders to be predictable, responsible, and credible. Failure to demonstrate consistency might lead to credibility crisis. Mahatma Gandhi maintained consistency throughout his life by sticking to non-violence and peace. He remarked, "True morality consists, not in following the beaten track, but in finding out the true path for ourselves and in fearlessly following it." Consistency is essential in every area of life. Consistency is essential in putting your efforts to achieve big. It is required to get noticed as a credible and responsible person.

Consideration

Consideration is one of the major characteristics of soft leaders as soft leaders basically care for their people. Consideration means how much and how far the leaders are sensitive towards their people. Leaders with consideration have more of people-orientation rather than task-orientation. They empathize with others and understand the problems. Mahatma Gandhi was an empathetic leader who always cared for and considered others. He said, "I don't believe in stereotypes, I prefer to hate people on a more personal basis. The measure of a truly great man is the courtesy with which he treats lesser men. An eye for an eye will make the whole world go blind."

Contribution

Contribution includes precious time, money, energy, ideas, knowledge, and service to the society. Genuine and selfless contribution takes to true leadership. People respect the leaders who contribute their best to the society without hankering for wealth, power, or prestige. Mahatma Gandhi said, "We must become the change we want to see in the world." His contribution to India's freedom movement, and to bring a qualitative difference in the lives of others is unquestionable. He enlightened the world with the knowledge that all religions in the world share common beliefs of truth and non-violence which is his major contribution to mankind. Here is the diagram connecting all 11C's that constitute soft leadership and symbolizes the characteristics of Mahatma Gandhi:

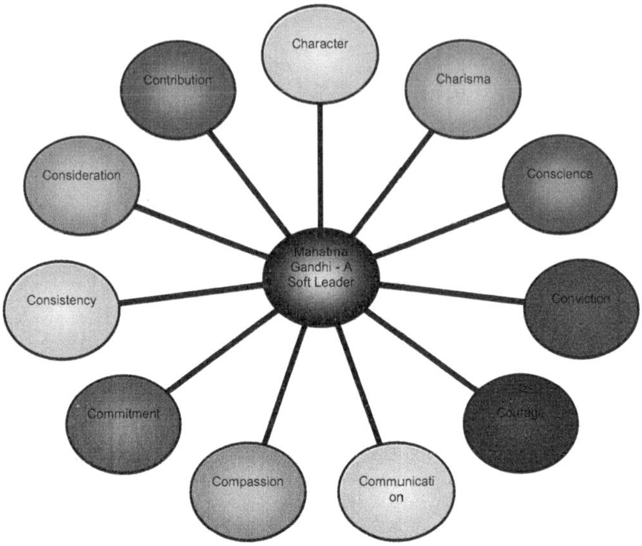

Mahatma Gandhi – A Soft Leader

Mahatma Gandhi said, "Truth and non-violence are as old as the hills. All I have done is to try experiments in both on as vast a scale as I could. In doing so, I have sometimes erred and learned by my errors. Life and its problems have thus become to me so many experiments in the practice of truth and nonviolence."

Mahatma Gandhi had more concern for people and was a participative, and relationship oriented leader. Commenting on leadership he quoted, "I suppose leadership at one time meant muscles; but today it means getting along with people." It clearly shows that his leadership style is closely connected with soft leadership. He provided a soft touch, believed in soft power, adopted soft tactics, and applied soft skills apart from possessing the 11 characteristics needed for a soft leader. Hence, we can conclude that Mahatma Gandhi was an ideal example for a soft leader. His principles are eternal and his leadership is everlasting.

Mahatma Gandhi continues to inspire people internationally through his soft leadership. He will be remembered as long as civilization exists. Present world needs another soft leader like Mahatma Gandhi to preach and practice non-violence and peace to eliminate intolerance and impatience, and to spread universal brotherhood and fraternity. Dr. Martin Luther King, Jr. said, "If humanity is to progress, Gandhi is inescapable. He lived, thought, acted and inspired by the vision of humanity evolving toward a world of peace and harmony."

Albert Einstein commented on Mahatma Gandhi as follows: "Generations to come, it may be, will scarce believe that such one as this ever in flesh and blood walked upon this earth."

References

http://www.emeraldinsight.com/journals.htm?articleid=1
7083779

http://onlinelibrary.wiley.com/doi/10.1002/ltl.20019/abs
tract

http://www.ila-
net.org/Webinars/Archive/Rao082012.html

Acknowledgement

Frances Hesselbein, President and CEO, Frances Hesselbein Leadership Institute

International Leadership Association

Appendix D

Soft Leadership – Webinar Q & A Session

"Curiosity has its own reason for existence. The important thing is not to stop questioning." - Albert Einstein

I led a webinar on "Soft Leadership: A New Leadership Perspective" organized by International Leadership Association on August 29, 2012. Here are some of the questions that came up from the participants during my webinar with my responses:

Q: What is Emerging as the Key Leadership Model for the Next Decade?

A: I have coined the term 'Soft Leadership' which is drawing attention internationally. It is going to prevail in future. This concept believes in partnership rather than followership. It believes in soft touch; adopts soft tactic; and practices soft skills to lead from the front to execute tasks successfully.

Q: What Kind of Leadership is Appropriate for the Speed and Complexity of Change that we Face Now?

A: Soft leadership helps greatly.

Q: What is Soft Leadership and its Relevance?

A: Soft leadership can be defined as the process of setting goals; influencing people through persuasion; building strong teams; negotiating them with a win-win attitude; respecting their failures; handholding them; motivating them constantly; aligning their energies and efforts; recognizing and appreciating their contribution in accomplishing organizational goals and objectives with an emphasis on soft skills. It is based on the right mindset, skill set, and toolset. This leadership style can be applied within the companies to achieve organizational excellence and effectiveness and within the countries to ensure global peace, prosperity and stability.

Q: Can You Elaborate on Soft Leadership?

Soft leadership is a new dimension to leadership. I coined this concept by blending several skills and abilities as there is a growing need for leaders to demonstrate this style with the changing times and technologies and global dynamic environment. It contains 11 C's such as character, charisma, conscience, conviction, courage, communication, compassion, commitment, consistency, consideration, and contribution. The same is represented by a diagram as follows:

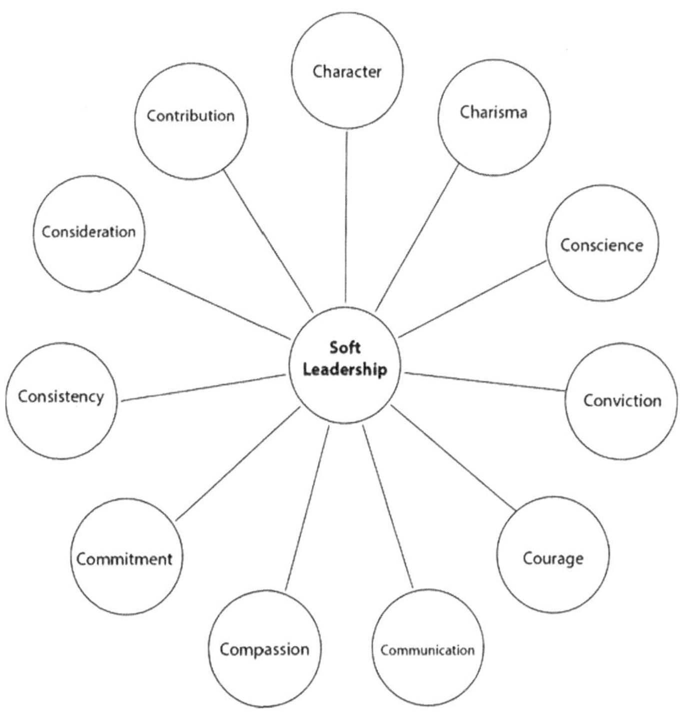

I requested Dave Ulrich, World's 23 Ranked Management Guru, and the Partner of The RBL Group to create a leadership code for Soft Leadership, and he was kind enough to interpret 11Cs and mapped onto the leadership code thus adding value to this leadership concept.

Soft leadership touches on caring, connecting, and communicating with people to accomplish desired goals. Soft leaders are basically people oriented rather than task oriented. They empathize with others and look at the issues from a human perspective. They have compassion towards others.

If the end of the 20th century belonged to emotional intelligence then the 21st century belongs to soft leadership where leaders have to demonstrate pleasing and polite behavior, attitude and personality to get the tasks executed by their partners. The 21st century also welcomes partnership replacing traditional leadership with followership attitude.

Q: Are all 11C's Imperative to Become a Soft Leader?

A: Ideally it is good to possess all 11 characteristics. But everybody cannot posses all these characteristics. If they possess the majority of them they can become soft leaders. They can develop the rest of the characteristics over a period time to excel as successful soft leaders. In a similar context, Daniel Goleman describes six leadership styles such as coaching leaders, pacesetting leaders, democratic leaders, affiliative leaders, authoritative leaders, and coercive leaders. He reveals that the leaders who master four or more leadership styles out of these six leadership styles and especially the democratic, authoritative, affiliative, and coaching styles can provide healthy workplace ambience thus achieving amazing performance from their group members.

Q: Is Diplomacy Part of Soft Leadership?

A: Diplomacy is different. I would like to put it in this manner: Soft leaders adopt soft tactics, soft methods, soft tools and techniques to get the tasks executed. They use soft skills to lead others. It is based on the right mindset, skill set and toolset. Globalization, liberalization, privatization and the rapid growth of technology have redefined the concept of leadership and role of leaders resulting in the need for a new and specialized set of skills that can be called soft leadership. I have coined this new leadership concept which is getting great response globally.

Soft leadership doesn't mean submissiveness or being soft physically, but being assertive where these leaders protect their rights without violating the rights of others. Soft leadership is not a submissive leadership or a lame duck leadership but an assertive leadership, and it is much beyond.

Soft leadership is all about influencing behavior and attitudes for collective good of the people. It includes trust, empathy, compassion and effective communication. It involves leadership related to people skills, interpersonal and communication skills. It can also be defined as the skills and abilities related to personality, attitude and behavior as that help in influencing the people while leading them.

There are 11 characteristics that distinguish soft leaders from others. They are character, charisma, conscience, conviction, courage, communication, compassion, commitment, consistency, consideration and contribution.

Q: What is the Role of Emotional Intelligence in Soft Leadership?

A: Emotional intelligence is a five-step process of discovering your emotions, managing your emotions, discovering the emotions of others, managing their emotions and motivating their emotions effectively. Emotional intelligence is essential irrespective of the leadership style as it is the basic ingredient of leadership. It is essential in higher degree in the case of soft leadership as this style emphasizes more on 'concern for people'.

Q: Do You Think Soft Leadership is Effective?

A: Yes very much. Soft leadership adopts soft skills, soft approach, soft tactics, and soft power to get the tasks executed successfully. Mahatma Gandhi is an apt example of soft leadership as he led India's independence through peace and non-violence when the entire world believed in the concept of 'might is right'. Hence, we don't have to doubt the effectiveness of soft leadership. In fact, it is soft leadership rather than hard leadership that is going to prevail in the years to come.

Q: You Mentioned Winston Churchill as an Example for one of the 11C's i.e. Communication. Do You Think he was a Soft Leader?

A: No, Winston Churchill was not a soft leader, but an assertive leader. I took him as an example because he inspired people with his communication skills during the Second World War and played a key role to ensure the victory of UK and other allied forces.

Q: You Highlight Soft Leadership only from the Perspective of Leadership. What about from the Perspective of Followership?

A: Soft leadership is all about leading people from the front with a soft approach. It believes in partnership rather than followership. Leaders exist as long as the partners exist. Hence, both leadership and partnership are two sides of the same coin. This concept dwells on changing the personality, attitude, and behavior of the people. It implies that it talks about the partners as well.

Q: Did You Develop any Innovative Tools for Soft Leadership?

A: I have developed a soft leadership grid connecting all 11 C's. I have been doing research on this style for quite a few years. In fact, my PhD thesis is on soft skills, and I integrated some of the best features of soft skills with this new concept. Dave Ulrich mapped the 11 C's onto the leadership code for this style on my request thus adding value to it. He also wrote the foreword for my book titled, *Soft Leadership: Make Others Feel More Important* which is generating great interest globally. I am still doing extensive research, and I am sure I will be able to create innovative tools and models to enhance credibility to my concept so that it is beneficial to both individuals and organizations. I would like all types of leaders to make use of this leadership style to ensure all-round peace and prosperity to mankind.

Q: What is Your Role as a Leadership Guru?

A: I am passionate about leadership. I do research round the clock to find out new leadership perspectives that are beneficial to leaders to make this world a better place to live. I author books and share my knowledge through workshops, seminars and training programs. My aim is to apply my leadership knowledge to ensure global stability, peace and prosperity.

Q: What is Your Vision?

A: I want to share my knowledge with the world. Hence, I created three blogs http://professormsraoguru.blogspot.com http://professormsrao.blogspot.com, http://profmsr.blogspot.com and a Facebook Page http://www.facebook.com/pages/Professor-MSRao/451516514937414?skip_nax_wizard=true to share my knowledge online and also through teaching and training programs. My long-term vision is to train 1,000,000 people and develop them as leaders. I want to make a difference in the lives of others and to the society as a whole. I want to promote global peace and prosperity. I want to apply "Soft Leadership" style in all areas to make people important and special so that they can wholeheartedly contribute for the benefit of mankind.

Q: What is Your Message to the World?

A: Love your mother, but don't hate another person's mother. Love your community but don't hate another person's community. Look at similarities, not differences. Above all, make a difference in the lives of others.

"Effective questioning brings insight, which fuels curiosity, which cultivates wisdom." - Chip Bell

References

http://speakermix.com/professor-m-s-rao
http://www.facebook.com/pages/Professor-MSRao/451516514937414?skip_nax_wizard=true
http://professormsraoguru.blogspot.com
http://professormsrao.blogspot.com
http://profmsr.blogspot.com
http://www.ila-net.org/Webinars/Archive/Rao082012.html
http://www.emeraldinsight.com/journals.htm?articleid=17083779

Note

The webinar generated great interest. The participants raised many questions but I could not respond to all questions due to paucity of time. Hence, I included the questions with answers in this appendix for the benefit of readers.

References

Start LD Early When is the Right Time? by Jack Zenger, Leadership Excellence April, 2013

Smart Leadership: Lessons for Leaders M.S.Rao (2012) Sterling Publishers

Success - What Every Leader Needs to Know, John C. Maxwell

Change Management – A guide to effective implementation authored by Robert A. Paton and James McCalman (Publishers - Response Books- Sage Publications)

Managing Organisational Change authored by V.Nilakant and S.Ramnarayan (Publishers - Response Books- Sage Publications)

Management Challenges for the 21st century by Peter Ferdinand Drucker

Online References

Author's Speakermix: http://speakermix.com/professor-m-s-rao

Author's Facebook Page: http://www.facebook.com/pages/Professor-MSRao/451516514937414?skip_nax_wizard=true

Author's Blog: http://profmsr.blogspot.com

Author's Blog: http://professormsrao.blogspot.com

Author's Blog: http://professormsraoguru.blogspot.com

http://www.amanet.org/training/books/9780814413388.a
spx

http://books.google.co.in/books?isbn=080101378X

www.rallabandi.in/downloads/Time_Management.pdf

www.abdulkalam.com

http://edition.presstv.ir/detail/127534.html

http://www.illinoishistory.gov/facsimiles.htm

http://www.ila-
net.org/Webinars/Archive/Rao082012.html

http://www.emeraldinsight.com/journals.htm?articleid=1
7083779

http://onlinelibrary.wiley.com/doi/10.1002/ltl.20019/abs
tract

Key Points

1. Believe in fraternity and universal brotherhood.
2. Start leadership development process early in the students.
3. Cultivate a unique mindset, toolset and skills set in students.
4. Assess your personality type to explore leadership opportunities.
5. Come out of your comfort zone to soar like an eagle.
6. Develop the 'I can make it happen' mindset.
7. Acquire "transferable skills" to fast-track your career.
8. Manage and master every moment in your life.
9. Prepare mentally to face corporate challenges to ensure your survival and success.
10. Build and protect your professional image.
11. Adopt the 'Mirroring Technique' to win friends and influence others.
12. Blend hard and soft skills to excel as a smart leader.
13. Embrace change to excel as an effective leader.
14. Compete with yourself to raise your bar constantly.

15. Emphasize on your efforts, and outcomes will follow accordingly.
16. Be employable and deployable to have a foothold in the corporate world.
17. Adopt 21 timeless tools to become a CEO quickly.
18. Acquire CEO acumen and learn the ropes of other departments to become a CEO.
19. Spot the right talent and build the leaders around you.
20. Achieve success with integrity.
21. Be proud of being an Indian.

Epilogue

"Character cannot be developed in ease and quiet. Only through experiences of trial and suffering can the soul be strengthened, vision cleared, ambition inspired and success achieved." - Helen Keller

I have authored this book to groom students as leaders and reach senior positions quickly. If this book helps you achieve your expectations, it will have done its job. If you put this book down feeling that you are better equipped to become a successful leader, I feel that my work as an author has been accomplished.

I would appreciate your valuable feedback to make improvements to this book. You may post your feedback at http://speakermix.com/professor-m-s-rao, Facebook Page: http://www.facebook.com/pages/Professor-MSRao/451516514937414?skip_nax_wizard=true or send me an email: profmsr13@gmail.com. If you want information on the seminars and workshops on leadership that I conduct or my availability as a speaker for your group or conference, please contact me. You may also visit my Blogs http://profmsr.blogspot.com, http://professormsrao.blogspot.com, and http://professormsraoguru.blogspot.com which are widely read globally. These blogs pertain to Learning, Leadership, Coaching, and Soft Skills. Please post your comments directly on the blogs themselves, as it helps others appreciate your ideas. If you find the blogs interesting, please share the links with your friends, as knowledge grows when shared.

You may share your thoughts about *Student Leaders: Growing From Students To CEOs* on Facebook, Twitter, LinkedIn, and the websites you visit. You can also blog about it or write a book review.

I pray for your success.

Professor M.S.Rao

Founder, MSR Leadership Consultants India

About The Author

Professor M.S.Rao,

International Leadership Guru

Blogs: http://profmsr.blogspot.com

http://professormsrao.blogspot.com

http://professormsraoguru.blogspot.com

Professor M.S.Rao is an international leadership guru who rose from humble origins. He is recognized as one of the world's leading leadership educators, authors, speakers, coaches, consultants and practitioners. He has 32 years of experience in leadership development, and conducts leadership development training programs for various corporates and educational institutions. He is a Success Coach and Motivational Speaker, and delivers guest lectures upon request. He coined a new leadership tool – *Soft Leadership Grid;* leadership teaching tool – *11E Leadership Grid;* and innovative teaching tool – *Meka's Method.* His areas of interest include Leadership, Coaching, and Learning and Development.

He is the Founder of MSR Leadership Consultants, India and the author of 21 books including the award-winning *21 Success Sutras for Leaders.* He has published more than 250 papers and articles in international publications including *Leader to Leader, Leadership Excellence, T+D Magazine (ASTD), Personal Excellence, Chief Learning Officer Magazine, Emerald,* and *Sage.* He serves as an Advisor and Board Member for several prestigious international organizations including American Institute of Business Psychology (AIOBP), USA. and Global Leadership Awards, Malaysia. He has been listed as one of the leading achievers around the world in *Marquis Who's Who in the World* in 2013. He successfully led a webinar as a thought leader on

Soft Leadership: A New Leadership Perspective organized by International Leadership Association, America.

He serves on the editorial boards of various prestigious international journals including *Development and Learning in Organizations* and *Industrial and Commercial Training* of Emerald Journals - U.K, *International Journal of Business Administration* - Canada, and *Journal of Business Studies Quarterly* - USA. He is ranked as No.1 among the speakers in India as per reviews on Speakermix.org URL: http://speakermix.com/professor-m-s-rao. He can be reached at: profmsr13@gmail.com and additionally maintains three popular blogs titled 'Where Knowledge is Wealth' - URL http://profmsr.blogspot.com 'Professor M.S.Rao Born for the Students' URL http://professormsrao.blogspot.com and 'Knowledge Grows When Shared'- URL http://professormsraoguru.blogspot.com

List of Books Published by the Author

1. 21 Success Sutras for Leaders
2. Smart Leadership: Lessons for Leaders
3. Success Can Be Yours
4. Spirit of Indian Youth: Soft Skills for Young Managers
5. Stand Out! Build a Successful Career and Become a Global Leader
6. Secrets of Your Leadership Success: The 11 Indispensable E's of a Leader
7. Sharpen Your Mind: Acquire Tools to Achieve Your Success
8. Strategies for Improving Your Business Communication: The Book for Leaders to Communicate and Achieve Professional Success

9. Soft Leadership: Make Others Feel More Important
10. Smartness Guide: Success Tools for Students
11. Soft Skills for Students: Classroom to Corporate
12. Sage Advice for Students and Educators: Stay Inspired!
13. Soup for Academic Leaders: Acquire Teaching Tools to Achieve Your Academic Leadership Success
14. Spot Your Leadership Style: Build Your Leadership Brand
15. Secrets for Success: Failure is only a Comma, Not a Full Stop
16. Soft Skills: Enhancing Employability
17. Success Tools for Freshers: Soar Like Eagles!

Shroff Reprints & Original Titles
The X Team Series
(An Imprint of Shroff Publishers)

Computers

ISBN	Title	Author	Year	Price
9789350236321	**.NET Interview Q&A, 164 Pages**	**Harwani**	**2012**	**225.00**
9789350237830	**Advanced Java for Students, 216 Pages**	**Mehta**	**2012**	**250.00**
9788184041569	Ajax for Beginners (B/CD), 452 Pages	Bayross	2006	375.00
9788184041972	Application Development with Oracle & PHP on Linux for Beginners, 2/ed (B/CD), 940 Pages	Bayross	2007	650.00
9789350233733	Blogging for Beginners, 268 Pages	Harwani	2011	350.00
9788184046397	C for Beginners, 532 Pages	Mothe	2009	400.00
9789350233900	C Interviews Q&A, 192 Pages	Thorat	2011	150.00
9789350238172	**C Interviews Q&A, 2nd Edition 244 Pages**	**Thorat**	**2012**	**225.00**
9788184046564	C++ for Beginners, 403 Pages	Harwani	2009	400.00
9789350231012	Core Java for Beginners, (B/CD), 892 Pages	Shah	2010	575.00
9788184046694	Database Concepts and Systems for Students, 3/ed, 428 Pgs	Bayross	2009	375.00
9789350239995	**E-Marketing for Beginners, 168 Pages**	**Gadkari**	**2013**	**250.00**
9788184047059	Hibernate 3 for Beginners - Covers Java Persistence API (B/CD), 680 Pages	Shah	2009	500.00
9788184048780	HTML for Beginners, 2nd Edition, 416 Pages	Aibara	2010	575.00
9789350236475	**HTML5 for Beginners, 564 Pages**	**Aibara**	**2012**	**450.00**
9788184045697	Java EE 5 for Beginners, Revised & Enlarged 2nd Edition (B/CD), 1,192 Pages	Bayross	2008	575.00
9788184049398	Java EE 6 for Beginners, (B/CD), 1092 Pages	Shah	2009	825.00
9788184049411	Java EE 6 Server Programming for Professionals (B/DVD), 1,328 Pages	Shah	2010	950.00
9788184048063	Java EE Project using EJB 3, JPA and Struts 2 for Beginners, (B/CD), 1258 Pages	Shah	2009	1,025.00
9789350237557	**Java for Beginners, 2nd Edition (B/CD), Covers Java SE 7 JDK, 576 Pgs**	**Chavan**	**2012**	**550.00**
9788184045932	Java for Professionals: A Practical Approach to Java Programming (Covers Java SE 6), 790 Pages	Harwani	2008	525.00
9789350233719	Java for Students, 2nd Edition, 850 Pages	Pherwani	2011	600.00
9788184047097	Java Persistence API in EJB 3 for Professionals, (B/CD) 756 Pgs	Shah	2009	550.00
9788184043594	Java Server Pages for Beginners (B/CD), 872 Pages	Bayross	2007	500.00
9788184045925	JavaServer Pages Project for Beginners, (B/CD), 746 Pages	Shah	2008	550.00
9788184048438	Lamp Programming for Professionals, (B/CD), 1,284	Shah	2009	975.00
9789350233986	**Mobile Computing for Beginners, 782 Pages**	**Shende**	**2012**	**750.00**
9788184040142	MySQL 5 for Professionals (B/CD), 770 Pages	Bayross	2005	550.00
9789350235188	MySQL 5.1 for professionals (B/CD), 772 Pages	Bayross	2011	650.00
9788184045260	Oracle for Professionals (Covers Oracle 9i, 10g & 11g) (B/CD), 1,420 Pgs	Shah	2008	975.00
9788184043228	PC Hardware for Beginners, 308 Pages	Sangia	2007	300.00
9788184040753	PHP 5.1 for Beginners (B/CD), 1,284 Pages	Bayross	2006	725.00
9788184048445	PHP Project for Beginners, (B/CD), 1,200 Pages	Shah	2011	600.00
9788184047073	Practical ASP.NET 3.5 Projects for Beginners, (B/CD), 550 Pgs	Harwani	2009	450.00

ISBN	Title	Author	Year	Price
9788184048070	Practical EJB Project for Beginners, 312 Pages	Harwani	2009	325.00
9788184043426	Practical Java Project for Beginners (B/CD), 164 Pages	Harwani	2007	175.00
9788184043419	Practical Web Services for Beginners, 168 Pages	Harwani	2007	150.00
9789350234907	Programming With PL/SQL for Beginners, 236 Pages	Patil	2011	300.00
9789350231241	QTP for Professionals, 480 Pages	Reddy	2010	450.00
9789350236499	**SAP MM for Beginners, 384 Pages**	**Rakshit**	**2012**	**525.00**
9789350233894	SAP SD for Beginners, 2/ed, 252 Pages	Samad	2011	350.00
9789350236482	**Software Automation Testing Tools for Beginners, 1,112 Pages**	**Shende**	**2012**	**1,000.00**
9789350231050	**Software Documentation for Professionals, 600 Pages**	**Shah**	**2012**	**450.00**
9789350236901	**Spring 3 for Beginners (Book/CD-Rom), 612 Pages**	**Shah**	**2012**	**575.00**
9789350237755	**Spring 3 with Hibernate 4 Project for Professionals, (B/DVD), 886 Pgs**	**Shah**	**2012**	**750.00**
9788184047448	Struts 2 for Beginners, 2/ed, (B/CD), 566 Pages	Shah	2009	525.00
9788184046960	Struts 2 with Hibernate 3 Project for Beginners, (B/CD), 1,042 Pages	Shah	2009	775.00
9788184041071	Visual Basic 2005 for Beginners (B/CD), 1,172 Pages	Bayross	2006	150.00

Other Computer Titles

ISBN	Title	Author	Year	Price
9789350230237	A Primer on Software Quality Models & Project Management, 640 Pgs	Mehta	2010	900.00
9788184048827	Art of Creative Destruction: Illustarted Software Testing & Test Automation....for the Testing Times, 2/ed, 248 Pages	Puranik	2010	425.00
9789350232859	Beginning Web Development for Smartphones Developing Web Applications with PHP, MySQL and jQTouch, 252 Pages	Harwani	2011	300.00
9789350237526	**Business @ Cloud Level, 272 Pages**	**Yadav**	**2012**	**425.00**
9789350231029	C# 4.0 Programming Made Easy, 624 Pages	Kadam	2011	425.00
9789350230244	Computer Architecture and Maintenance, 320 Pages	Kadam	2010	250.00
9789350235553	Data Structure and Algorithm, 492 Pages	Rukadikar	2011	400.00
9788184048957	FAQ's in MFC and MFC Solutions, Vol I (B/CD), 510 Pages	P. G. Naik	2010	425.00
9788173666810	First Encounter with Java Including BlueJ, 386 Pages	Bhutta	2006	225.00
9789350230275	Instant Oracle, 100 Pages	Shah	2010	75.00
9788173664632	Introducing MySQL, 96 Pages	Oak	2005	50.00
9789350230251	Management Information System (MIS), 176 Pages	Kadam	2010	200.00
9789350231258	Maximum Oracle with Oracle Best Practices, 772 Pages	Puranik	2011	675.00
9788184043402	Operating Systems, 376 Pages	Sumitradevi	2008	300.00
9788184047899	Operating Systems, 2/ed, 408 Pages	Sumitradevi	2009	400.00
9789350234242	Oracle Financials 11i: A Practical Guide for the Beginners, 392 Pages	Peri	2011	725.00
9789350236918	**Oracle Financials 11i, 2/ed: A Practical Guide for the Beginners, 436 Pages**	**Peri**	**2012**	**725.00**
9788173668012	Software Defect Prevention Concepts and Implementation, 180 Pages (H/B)	Kane & Bajaj	2003	300.00
9789350236307	**Software Testing: Interview Questions, 176 Pages**	**Reddy**	**2012**	**175.00**
9788173668814	Strategic Bidding: A Successful Approach (for IT / Consultancy), 192 Pgs	Garg	2004	275.00
9789350237120	**Testing in 30+ Open Source Tools, 2nd Edition, (B/CD), 1,340 Pages**	**Shende**	**2013**	**975.00**
9788173660429	Vijay Mukhi's ERP Odyssey: Implementing. PeopleSoft Financials 7.0/7.5, 528 Pages	Mukhi	1999	350.00

Business, Management & Finance

ISBN	Title	Author	Year	Price
9789350238936	**100% Forex Learning and Earning (Natural Shade Paper Use) 236 Pages**	**Darazhanov**	**2012**	**275.00**
9788184046977	An Introduction to Foreign Exchange & Financial Risk Management, (B/CD), 348 Pages	Lakshman	2009	400.00

ISBN	Title	Author	Year	Price
9789350230268	Bootstrapping A Software Company, 348 Pages	Yadav	2010	425.00
9788184044249	Break Your Negative Attitude, 114 Pages	Dr. Mishra	2007	125.00
9788184040425	Developing Analytical Skills: Case Studies in Management, 636 Pages	Dr. Natarajan	2008	500.00
9788173660993	Doing Business with the French, 150 Pages	Jhangiani	1999	150.00
9788184044959	Enabling Event-ful Experiences, 250 Pages	Balachandran	2008	200.00
9789350237380	**Ethical Supply Chain Management in India, 124 Pages**	**Fernandes**	**2012**	**200.00**
9788184044744	Ethics, Indian Ethos and Management, 2nd/Ed 252 Pages	Balachandran	2008	175.00
9789350231227	Financial Decision Modeling Operations Research & Business Statistics, 696 Pages	Sridhar	2010	350.00
9789350238929	**Financial Management: Problems & Solutions, 5/ed, 1,228 Pgs**	**Sridhar**	**2012**	**950.00**
9789350237540	**Fixed Income Markets in India: Investment Opportunities for You, 280 Pgs**	**Sen**	**2012**	**350.00**
9789350239728	**Fixed Income Markets in India: Investment Opportunities for You, (2 Colour) 280 Pages**	**Apte**	**2013**	**750.00**
9789351100102	**Funding Techniques of World Renowned Universities, 204 Pgs**	**Dharaskar**	**2013**	**500.00**
9789350232965	Futures & Options: Equities-Trading Strategies & Skills, 4/ed, 392 Pages	Sridhar	2011	475.00
9789350233917	Globally Distributed Work, 276 Pages	Mehta	2011	425.00
9789350233887	Hospitality Management, 476 Pages	Shirke	2011	525.00
9788184040432	How to Eat The Elephant? The CEO's Guide To An Enterprise Sys Implementation, 104 Pages	Tulsyan	2007	325.00
9789350233108	How to Learn Management from your wife (HB), 96 Pages	Rangnekar	2011	275.00
9789350230459	How to Learn Management from your wife (PB), 96 Pages	Rangnekar	2010	125.00
9788184044164	Logistics in International Business, 2/ed, 428 Pages	Aserkar	2007	450.00
9788184047547	Magic and Logic of Elliott Waves, The, 204 Pages	Kale	2009	500.00
9788184048568	Management Accounting & Financial Analysis for C.A.Final (June 2009), 9/ed, 540 Pages	Sridhar	2009	400.00
9789350235126	Management of Services, 348 Pages	Poddar	2011	450.00
9788184047066	Purchasing and Inventory Management, 338 Pages	Menon	2009	475.00
9789350233870	Quantitative Techniques for Project Management, 268 Pages	Velayoudam	2011	600.00
9788173666797	Rules of Origin in International Trade, 238 Pages	Dr. Sathpathy	2005	300.00
9789350233580	Services Marketing, 448 Pages	Balachandran	2011	425.00
9789350233115	Soft Skills In Management, 148 Pages	Rangnekar	2011	175.00
9788173668814	Strategic Bidding: A Successful Approach (for IT / Consultancy), 192 Pages	Garg	2004	275.00
9789351101123	**Strategic Financial Management for C.A. Final, 11/ed 800 Pages**	**Sridhar**	**2013**	**695.00**
9789351100096	**Strategic Financial Management, C. A. Final,Revision Book, 2/ed, 320 Pgs**	**Sridhar**	**2013**	**250.00**
9789350239438	Strategies For Improving Your Business Communication, 196 Pages	Rao	2012	250.00
9788184043211	Time Your Trades With Technical Analysis (B/CD), 348 Pages	Pradhan	2007	600.00

Catering & Hotel Management

ISBN	Title	Author	Year	Price
9788173668739	Careers in Hospitality - Hotel Management Entrance Exam Guide, 332 Pages	Rego	2004	200.00
9789350238103	**Food and Beverage Management, 524 Pages**	**Shirke**	**2013**	**700.00**
9789350239537	**Food Production and Culinary Art, 524 Pages**	**Verma**	**2013**	**700.00**
9789350233887	Hospitality Management, 476 Pages	Shirke	2011	525.00
9789350238158	**Marvels of Indian Jam, Juice, Sauce, Salad &....., 190 Pages**	**Shankaran**	**2012**	**250.00**
9789350238141	**Marvels of Indian Pickles, Chutneys and Condiments, 124 Pgs**	**Shankaran**	**2012**	**200.00**
9789350230817	Marvels of Indian Snacks, 264 Pages	Shankaran	2011	350.00
9789350238189	**Marvels of Indian Sweets, 152 Pages**	**Shankaran**	**2012**	**250.00**
9788184046687	Marvels of North Indian Cuisine, 196 Pages	Shankaran	2009	325.00
9788184044751	Marvels of South Indian Cuisine, 220 Pages	Shankaran	2008	250.00

Civil Engineering

ISBN	Title	Author	Year	Price
9789350233252	Concrete for High Performance Sustainable Infrastructure, 312 Pages	Dhir	2011	750.00
9789350233245	New Developments in Concrete Construction, 296 Pages	Dhir	2011	750.00
9788184043785	Raina's Concrete Bridge Practice, 3/ed : Analysis,			

ISBN	Title	Author	Year	Price
	Design & Economics, 856 Pages	Dr. Raina	2007	TBA
9788184048056	Raina's Concrete Bridge Practice: Construction, Maintenance and Rehabiliation 2/ed, 452 Pages (H/B) [14 Full Color Inserts]	Dr. Raina	2010	625.00
9788184048049	Raina's Concrete Bridge: Inspection, Repair, Strengthening, Testing, Load Capacity Evaluation 2/ed, 800 Pages (H/B) [32 Full Color Inserts]	Dr. Raina	2010	800.00
9788184047530	Raina's Concrete for Construction: Facts and Practice, 400 Pages (H/B)	Dr. Raina	2009	650.00
9788184047875	Raina's Construction & Contract Management, 2/ed Inside Story, 585 Pages (H/B)	Dr. Raina	2009	850.00
9788184046618	Raina's Field Manual for Highway and Bridge Engineers, 3/ed, 1,404 Pgs	Dr. Raina	2009	1,800.00
9789350231418	**Raina's Handbook For Concrete Bridges, (Set of 2 Volumes), 2088 Pgs**	**Dr. Raina**	**2012**	**8000.00**
9788184040135	The World of Bridges, 300 Pages (H/B) [4 color]	Dr. Raina	2006	1,000.00
9789350231180	Using Primavera 6: Planning, Executing, Monitoring and Controlling Projects, 228 Pages	Al-Saridi	2010	350.00

Chartered Accountancy

ISBN	Title	Author	Year	Price
9789350231227	Financial Decision Modeling Operations Research & Business Statistics, 696 Pages	Sridhar	2010	350.00
9788184048568	Management Accounting & Financial Analysis for C.A.Final (June 2009), 9/ed, 540 Pages	Sridhar	2009	400.00
9789351101123	**Strategic Financial Management for C.A. Final, 11/ed 800 Pages**	**Sridhar**	**2013**	**695.00**

Communication

ISBN	Title	Author	Year	Price
9788184047905	Enhancing Soft Skills, 346 Pages	Biswas	2009	400.00
9789350231265	Knowing Your Words Worth: A Practical Guide to Communicating Effectively in English, 180 Pages	Shirodkar	2011	225.00
9789350239438	**Strategies For Improving Your Business Communication, 196 Pages**	**Rao**	**2012**	**250.00**

Dental / Health / Medical

ISBN	Title	Author	Year	Price
9789351100027	**Cancer: A Comma, not a Fullstop, 196 Pages**	**Venkatesh**	**2013**	**275.00**
9789351100485	**My Family Doctor, 176 Pages**	**Dr. Gadkari**	**2013**	**200.00**
9788173660986	Notes on Pathology, 11th Millennium Edition, 482 Pages	Experienced Prof.	2000	350.00
9788173668975	Splinting Management of MOBILE & Migrating Teeth, 104 Pgs	Dr. Kakar	2004	150.00
9788173669798	The Balancing Act "A Win Over Obesity", 296 Pages	Dr. Gadkari	2005	225.00
9788184049480	The Balancing Act "Know Your Heart", 368 Pages	Dr. Gadkari	2010	325.00

Economics

ISBN	Title	Author	Year	Price
9788184043266	Analysing Macroeconomics: A Toolkit for Managers, Executives & Students (Hardback), 156 Pages	Rakesh Singh	2007	500.00
9788184044171	Analysing Macroeconomics: A Toolkit for Managers, Executives & Students (Paperback), 156 Pages	Rakesh Singh	2007	250.00
9789350239124	Regional Trade Agreements, 320 Pages	Kamat	2013	750.00
9788173666797	Rules of Origin in International Trade, 238 Pages	Dr. Sathpathy	2005	300.00

Electrical Engineering

ISBN	Title	Author	Year	Price
9788184043235	Basic Electrical Circuits, 2/ed, 368 Pages	Dr. Salam	2007	250.00

Electronics & Communication

ISBN	Title	Author	Year	Price
9788173669002	Electronic Components and Materials, 3/ed, 404 Pages	Joshi	2004	175.00

Electronics & Engineering

ISBN	Title	Author	Year	Price
9788173663772	Principles of Environmental Science Engineering and Maintenance, 288 Pages	Dr. Thirumurthy	2004	175.00

ISBN	Title	Author	Year	Price
Event Management				
9788184044959	Enabling Event-ful Experiences, 250 Pages	Balachandran	2008	250.00
General Titles				
9788184045642	Hello Police Station (Marathi), 118 Pages	Shinde	2008	100.00
9789350232910	**Kuch Main Bhi Kahoon, 250 Pages**	**Subbu**	**2012**	**295.00**
9789350231760	Mom Don't Spoil Me, 140 Pages	Dr. C. S. Mishra	2010	150.00
9789350236338	Residential Interior Design for the Elderly and Physically Challenged, 200 Pages	Ray	2012	450.00
HRD				
9788184047080	Departmental Enquiries: Concept, Procedure & Practice, 534 Pages	Goel	2009	475.00
9788184040425	Developing Analytical Skills: Case Studies in Management, 636 Pgs	Dr. Natarajan	2008	500.00
9788184044744	Ethics, Indian Ethos and Management, 2nd/Ed 252 Pages	Balachandran	2008	175.00
9788184046229	How To Improve Trainer Effectiveness, 170 Pages	Balachandran	2008	200.00
International Trade				
9789350239124	**Regional Trade Agreements, 320 Pages**	**Kamat**	**2013**	**750.00**
Law				
9789350230800	A Handbook on the Maintenance & Welfare of Parents and Senior Citizens Act, 2007., 160 Pages	Gracias	2010	150.00
9788173664151	Customs Valuation in India 3/ed, 262 Pages	Satapathy	2002	375.00
9788173661426	Law of Sale of Goods & Partnership, 228 Pages	Chandiramani	2000	150.00
9788184042481	Laws of Carriage of Goods By Sea & Multimodal Transport In India, 92 Pages	Hariharan	2007	60.00
9788173666797	Rules of Origin in International Trade, 238 Pages	Dr. Sathpathy	2005	300.00
9789350231289	Social Security, Insurance and the Law, 460 Pages	Gopalakrishna	2011	600.00
Learning Disability				
9789350233924	On the wave of Brain: A Broad Perspective of Learning Disability 300 Pages	Jain	2011	450.00
Marine				
9788184043242	Containerisation, Multimodal Transport and Infrastructure			
9788173665516	A Textbook on Container & Multimodal Transport Management, 522 Pgs	Dr. Hariharan	2002	600.00
9788184043242	Containerisation, Multimodal Transport and Infrastructure Development in India, 5/ed, 852 Pages	Hariharan	2007	650.00
9788184043136	Marine Control Technology, 336 Pages	Majumder	2007	425.00
9788173669279	Marine Diesel Engines, 428 Pages	Aranha	2004	250.00
9789350238905	Marine Electrical Technology, 6/ed, 1,180 Pages	Fernandes	2013	950.00
9788173660801	Marine Internal Combustion Engines, 272 Pages	Kane	2003	275.00
9788173661419	Maritime Education, Training & Assessment Manual (TAP) - Vol II, 474 Pages,	DG Shipping	1999	400.00
9788173660375	Merchant Shipping: (STCW) Rules, 1998 incl. Training & Assessment Programme - 1,216 Pages	DG Shipping	1998	225.00
Mathematics				
9789350236796	Graph Theory with Applications, 812 Pages	Dey	2012	300.00
Mechanical Engineering				
9789350236192	Glance On Transformer Oil, A 96 Pages	Pandey	2012	125.00

ISBN	Title	Author	Year	Price
Media				
9789351100249	Media Madness & The Awesome 3Some - Main Anjaani, 156 Pages	Kapoor	2013	175.00
Mobile Computing				
9789350232859	Beginning Web Development for Smartphones Developing Web Applications with PHP, MySQL and JqTouch, 252 Pages	Harwani	2011	300.00
9789350233986	Mobile Computing for Beginners, 1,059 Pages	Shende	2012	750.00
Motivation				
9788184044249	Break Your Negative Attitude, 114 Pages	Dr. Mishra	2007	125.00
9788173665271	Heads You Win, Tails You Win, 2/ed, 200 Pages	Dr.Mishra	2005	200.00
9789350236208	Life is Fundamentally Management!, 200 Pages	Senthival	2012	250.00
9789350230206	Nothing Is Absolute, 274 Pages	Balachandran	2010	300.00
9789350238080	Skills for your Career Success: Touch your Tipping Point, 135 Pages	Sai	2012	175.00
9789350238134	White Magique, 124 Pages	Herekar	2012	200.00
Parenting				
9789350231760	Mom Don't Spoil Me, 140 Pages	Dr. C. S. Mishra	2010	150.00
Patent				
9788184047882	Breeding Innovation and Intellectual Capital, 2/ed 196 Pgs	Dr.Batra	2009	750.00
Physics				
9788184043259	Gravitation Demythicised: An Introduction to Einstein's General Relativity and Cosmology for Common Man, 258 Pages	Shenoy	2007	250.00
9788184047929	Study Aid Theoretical Physics - Volume I: Relativistic Theory and Electrodynamics, 418 Pgs	Prof Fai	2010	475.00
9788184047912	Theoretical Physics - Volume I: Relativistic Theory and Electrodynamics, 490 Pages	Prof Fai	2010	650.00
Project Management / Software Engineering				
9789350230237	A Primer on Software Quality Models & Project Management, 640 Pages	Mehta	2010	900.00
9788184048568	Management Accounting & Financial Analysis for C.A.Final (June 2009), 9/ed, 540 Pages	Sridhar	2009	400.00
9789350233870	Quantitative Techniques for Project Management, 268 Pages	Velayoudam	2011	600.00
Self-Help				
9789350239674	Academic Excellence, 236 Pages	Shetty	2013	300.00
9788184047905	Enhancing Soft Skills, 346 Pages	Biswas	2009	400.00
9789350237113	Secrets of Your Leadership Success: The 11 Indispensable E's of a Leader, 212 Pages	Rao	2012	350.00
9789350238165	Sharpen Your Mind, 242 Pages	Rao	2012	350.00
9789350237533	Smart Moves Great Career, 148 Pages	Rastogi	2012	150.00

- **All Prices are in Indian Rupees**
- **Titles Released after January 2012 are marked in Bold.**